THE SALVATION ARMY

MANUAL OF SALVATIONISM

(Students' Book)

Based on original text

by

Colonel Milton S. Agnew (R), BS, BD

Revision approved by:
The Commissioners' Conference
Verona, New Jersey
May, 1985

The Manual of Salvationism
Copyright © 1968 by The Salvation Army

Revised - October, 1978
Revised - May, 1985

Library of Congress catalog card number: 68-22790

Instructors' Kit prepared by Charlene Pearson

All Scripture quotations (except where otherwise indicated in the text) have been taken from the *New International Version* of the Bible, copyright © 1978 by New York International Bible Society. Used by permission.

Permission to quote from *The New Testament in Modern English,* translated by J. B. Phillips, has been granted by the MacMillan Company; from the *Amplified New Testament* by Zondervan Publishing House; and from the *Good News Bible,* the Bible in Today's English Version. Copyright © American Bible Society, 1976.

CONTENTS

Students' Book

MANUAL OF SALVATIONISM

INTRODUCTION

What are the basic beliefs of The Salvation Army? What is its history? What are its activities? What place does it have among the churches of the world? What does it truly mean to be a Salvationist?

These and other questions have been *answered* in this brief manual. There have been, however, many questions *raised*. For example, what would happen to Christianity if the Bible were to be suddenly taken away? How does the kind of god that people worship affect them? Why do you suppose God wanted Jesus to come into this world in human form? What is the difference between mistakes and sins? What do we mean by the term "born again"? Why do you suppose there are so many denominations today? What does the name "The Salvation Army" really mean?

Between the questions answered and the questions raised, there should be some interesting and informative classes during the weeks to come. All recruits are welcomed to this course which is designed to stimulate your thinking and give you opportunity to ask questions and, with other members of the class, to "think through" on many interesting and important subjects.

You will note that unless otherwise indicated, all Scriptures from the Old and New Testaments have been taken from the *New International Version* (NIV) of the Bible—this is the case in both the instructors' and the students' books.

The lesson content in both books is the same, but additional information and extra material have been included in the instructors' books, and these pages have been identified by numbers *and* letters; e.g., 6a, 6b, 11a, 11b, etc.

FOREWORD

This *Manual of Salvationism* will, it is hoped, serve more than one purpose. It should be used as basic lesson material for the series of weekly Recruits' Preparation Classes which are held throughout the territory, usually during the first quarter of the year.

The manual is also intended to provide for the Salvationist a basic and simple statement of the faith to which he subscribes. Every Salvationist should possess a copy, so that, whether in classes of instruction, through soldiers' meetings, or by personal study, he may be *"ready always to give an answer to every man that asketh you a reason of the hope that is in you"* (1 Peter 3:15 *KJV*). In a day of theological confusion this is sorely needed.

The Recruits' Preparation Class should be established in every corps, and should be conducted by the corps officer, or other selected, qualified leader.

All persons who are 13 years of age and over, connected with The Salvation Army and not already senior soldiers, whether saved or not, should be considered as potential members for this class. Those who should particularly be included are junior soldiers (13 years of age or older) and senior recruits. Indeed, every recruit, whether junior or senior, must have the benefit of this course before being enrolled as a senior soldier.

While public enrollments should be planned for Easter Sunday when possible, it may be necessary to schedule a second series of classes during the autumn months for additional enrollments at that time.

The purposes for which the class should be held may be stated as follows:

1. To give instruction concerning the duties and privileges of senior soldiership in The Salvation Army.
2. To afford opportunity for recruits to make definite decisions and commitments to God and the Army in becoming senior soldiers of The Salvation Army.
3. To bring about a definite experience of salvation to any recruit who may still be unsaved.

THE DOCTRINES OF THE SALVATION ARMY

(As set forth in the Salvation Army Act 1980, Schedule 1)

1. We believe that the Scriptures of the Old and New Testaments were given by inspiration of God, and that they only constitute the Divine rule of Christian faith and practice.

2. We believe that there is only one God, who is infinitely perfect, the Creator, Preserver, and Governor of all things, and who is the only proper object of religious worship.

3. We believe that there are three persons in the Godhead—the Father, the Son and the Holy Ghost, undivided in essence and co-equal in power and glory.

4. We believe that in the person of Jesus Christ the Divine and human natures are united, so that He is truly and poperly God and truly and properly man.

5. We believe that our first parents were created in a state of innocency, but by their disobedience they lost their purity and happiness, and that in consequence of their fall all men have become sinners, totally depraved, and as such are justly exposed to the wrath of God.

6. We believe that the Lord Jesus Christ has by His suffering and death made an atonement for the whole world so that whosoever will may be saved.

7. We believe that repentance towards God, faith in our Lord Jesus Christ, and regeneration by the Holy Spirit, are necessary to salvation.

8. We believe that we are justified by grace through faith in our Lord Jesus Christ and that he that believeth hath the witness in himself.

9. We believe that continuance in a state of salvation depends upon continued obedient faith in Christ.

10. We believe that it is the privilege of all believers to be wholly sanctified, and that their whole spirit and soul and body may be preserved blameless unto the coming of our Lord Jesus Christ.

11. We believe in the immortality of the soul; in the resurrection of the body; in the general judgment at the end of the world; in the eternal happiness of the righteous; and in the endless punishment of the wicked.

SOLDIERS OF CHRIST—
THE BIBLICAL BASIS FOR
SALVATION ARMY SOLDIERSHIP

The picture of a Christian as a soldier is one of the most vivid metaphors in the New Testament. It is easy to understand how the image of soldiery readily came to the mind of Paul and the other apostles when we consider that they were daily summoned to engage in spiritual and, at times, physical conflict with Satan and his forces.

Imprisoned in Rome for the second and final time, facing imminent death at the hand of the insane Emperor Nero, the battle-weary Apostle Paul wrote a final letter to his young friend, Timothy. Knowing the struggles Timothy was encountering in pastoring the Ephesian Church, the veteran warrior encouraged him with these words: *"Endure hardship... like a good soldier of Christ Jesus. No one serving as a soldier gets involved in civilian affairs—he wants to please his commanding officer"* (2 Timothy 2:3,4).

Modern-day Christians still are enlisted by "the Captain of our salvation" (Hebrews 2:10, *KJV*) to fight the forces of darkness. As soldiers we are called to:

Enlistment—Enlistment is the initial step to becoming a soldier. The person who is seeking soldiership in God's army must first of all make a decision to join. There is no conscription; no one is drafted. A Christian is one who has made a conscious decision to accept Christ as Saviour and follow Him as a disciple. Joshua's words of challenge to the Children of Israel must be affirmed by every Christian recruit: *"... Choose for yourselves this day whom you will serve ... as for me and my household, we will serve the Lord"* (Joshua 24:15).

Obedience—Jesus said, *"If you obey My commands, you will remain in My love ... You are My friends if you do what I command"* (John 15:10,14).

Loyalty— The Apostle John tells us in Revelation 2:10, *"Do not be afraid of what you are about to suffer ... Be faithful, even to the point of death, and I will give you the crown of life."* The Lord's soldier is called to a life of faithfulness and loyalty. His loyalty is to Jesus Christ alone.

Discipline— *"Do your best to present yourself to God as one approved, a workman who does not need to be ashamed and who correctly handles the word of truth"* (2 Timothy 2:15).

1

Battle—	*"Fight the good fight of faith"* (1 Timothy 6:12). *" . . . (I) urge you to contend for the faith that was once for all entrusted to the saints"* (Jude 3). *"For our struggle is not against flesh and blood, but against the rulers, against the authorities, against the powers of this dark world and against the spiritual forces of evil in the heavenly realms"* (Ephesians 6:12).
Victory—	*" . . . Thanks be to God! He gives us the victory through our Lord Jesus Christ"* (1 Corinthians 15:57). Jesus promised, *"In this world you will have trouble. But take heart! I have overcome the world"* (John 16:33).

It is important for the Christian soldier to understand that the Captain of our salvation not only gained the victory for us, but He also provides the spiritual armor needed for the daily battles of life. Paul admonishes the Christian to *"put on the full armor of God so that you can take your stand against the devil's schemes"* (Ephesians 6:11). Divine armor is essential because the Christian faces a formidable, supernatural foe (Ephesians 6:12).

The Christian's armor (Ephesians 6:10-20) includes:

The belt of truth (v.14)—It is from the soldier's belt that his sword hangs, allowing him a freedom of movement while keeping his weapon close at hand.

The breastplate of righteousness (v.14)—A righteous life is the Christian soldier's primary defense.

The sandals (v.15)—A soldier with his sandals on is ready to move. The Christian is always ready and eager to share the gospel with all whom he meets.

The shield of faith (v.16)—The word Paul uses here describes an oblong shield which only heavily armored soldiers carried—not the small, round conventional shield. This large shield was made of sectioned wood. It was pitch-soaked, and when fiery darts were thrown, the defender would duck behind his shield, and the darts would sink into the wood, extinguishing the flame. Only faith can protect the Christian from the darts of temptation.

The helmet of salvation (v.17)—Salvation protects both the front and the rear—the past, present, and future. Christ's salvation forgives past sins and gives strength to conquer sin in the future.

The sword of the Spirit (v.17)—The Word of God is both a *defensive* and an *offensive* weapon. It is a defense against sin and a weapon of attack against the sins of this world.

2

Prayer (v.18)—Here is the greatest weapon of them all! Paul notes that the Christian soldier's prayer life must be constant; it must be *intense;* and it must be *unselfish.*

Salvationists are soldiers of Jesus Christ. We are engaged in a continual battle against Satan for the souls of men. *The Christian Mission Magazine* of September 1878 stated that the Mission "has organized a Salvation Army to carry the blood of Christ and the fire of the Holy Ghost to every corner of the world." For more than 100 years Salvationists around the world have followed the biblical command to *"endure hardship with us like a good soldier of Christ Jesus"* (2 Timothy 2:3). They have gladly put on the armor of God and are actively fighting the battle for souls. With Christ as their Captain, Salvationists join their conquering Christian brothers and sisters in singing and believing these great words:

> *Soldiers of Christ, arise,*
> *And put your armor on,*
> *Strong in the strength which God supplies*
> *Through His eternal Son.*
> *Strong in the Lord of hosts,*
> *And in His mighty power,*
> *Who in the strength of Jesus trusts*
> *Is more than conqueror.*
> —*Charles Wesley*

STUDENTS' REVIEW
LESSON 1

1. List the armor described by the prophet Isaiah in 59:17:
    a. _____
    b. _____
    c. _____
    d. _____

2. a. What does Psalm 34:7 promise to those who "fear the Lord?"
    _____
    _____

    b. If you were to believe this with all your heart, how would this affect your life? _____
    _____

3. a. Each of the following verses describes a quality of spiritual armor. Name each:
    1. Romans 13:12   Armor of _____
    2. 2 Corinthians 6:7   Armor of _____
    3. Ephesians 6:13   Armor of _____
    4. 1 Thessalonians 5:8   Breastplate of _____ and
    _____
    5. 1 Thessalonians 5:8   Helmet of _____

    b. Think about each type of armor just listed. Have you heeded God's Word and put on the types of armor suggested? What do you think would happen in our world if many more people were to "put on the whole armor of God?"

4. How is the Christian's spiritual warfare described in the following verses?
    a. 1 Timothy 6:12   "The good fight of _____."
    b. 1 Peter 5:8   "Be _____, be _____."
    c. 1 Peter 2:11   "Abstain from _____ which war against the soul."

5. How is victory described in the following verses?
    a. 1 Corinthians 15:57   Victory is from _____
    b. Romans 7:24,25   Victory is through _____
    c. 1 John 5:4,5   Victory is by _____
    d. Romans 7:24,25   Victory is over _____
    e. Romans 16:20   Victory is over _____
    f. 1 Corinthians 15:54,55   Victory is over _____
    g. Romans 8:37   Victory is through _____

4

LESSON 2

GOD'S GREAT MESSAGE TO MAN

The best way to remember facts, history, and people is to have the information in writing. That is why we have books and libraries, and that is why we have the Bible. God knew that man needed a permanent, reliable record of many facts regarding Himself, the world, humankind, and His plan for people, so He arranged for these facts to be recorded. This record is know as the Bible, or the *Scriptures*. Because of the importance of God's written message to mankind, The Salvation Army has as its first doctrine a statement about the Bible. We are going to consider that statement in this lesson.

OUR FIRST DOCTRINE

This statement is the first of the eleven articles of Salvation Army belief because the Bible is the source from which all our doctrine comes:

> *We believe that the Scriptures of the Old and New Testaments were given by inspiration of God; and that they only constitute the Divine rule of Christian faith and practice.*

1. *The Scriptures:* The word *Scripture* means *writing,* and it is usually used in the plural, often with the word "holy." *Bible* means *book.* Look at Matthew 21:42 and Romans 1:2 which speak of "the Scriptures" and "the holy Scriptures," both of which refer to the *Old* Testament. Early in the life of the Christian Church these same titles were also given to the writings of the *New Testament.* In 2 Peter 3:15,16, Peter declared that some "ignorant and unstable people" treated Paul's writings with the same abuse which they gave to "the other Scriptures." Peter quite evidently classifies these letters of Paul as among "the Scriptures."[1]

2. *The Old and New Testaments:* These are the two major divisions of the Bible, with 39 books in the Old Testament and 27 in the New.[2] A "testament" is a covenant or an agreement. In the Old Testament, God covenants to provide a redeemer, and in the New Testament, He shows how that covenant was fulfilled in the person of Jesus Christ.[3a,3b] Jesus claimed that He was the redeemer promised in the Old Covenant: *"These are the Scriptures that testify about Me"* (John 5:39).

Also see Luke 24:13-27, 44-48; Isaiah 9:6,53; Psalm 110:1.[4]

3. *Language of the Scriptures:* The Old Testament was originally written in Hebrew; the New Testament in Greek.[5] The books of the Old and New Testaments are arranged in seven groups, not always in chronological order, but by style and content.

4. *Inspiration of the Scriptures:* In a library when we are referred

---

*These numbers refer to additional material in the instructors' *Manual of Salvationism*.

5

to a textbook or a resource book, we should know something of its author and its reliability. This is why we declare confidently: "The Scriptures of the Old and New Testaments were given by inspiration of God." The Scriptures were not thought up by clever men but they were committed to men by God the Holy Spirit.

Peter said: *"For no prophetic message ever came just from the will of man, but men were under the control of the Holy Spirit as they spoke the message that came from God"* (2 Peter 1:21, GBN). Peter is saying that God the Holy Spirit is actually the author of the Scriptures. The writers were not necessarily clever; in fact, many of them were quite ordinary people. But God chose "holy" men for this purpose. And they were "moved" or "carried along" or "impelled" by the Holy Spirit. That is, God gave very positive guidance to their thoughts, their messages, their speech, and their words. Holy men were fitted and guided by the Holy Spirit to receive and record truth as revealed to them by God. Maybe at times you have been "inspired" or "carried along" to write a poem or a letter. Scriptures, however, are inspired in a much deeper sense than that.[6]

"All Scripture is God-breathed" (2 Timothy 3:16) literally means that God "breathed" into all Scriptures.[7] Thus, both the Bible writers and the Bible itself are "God-breathed" or inspired. Consequently, the Book comes to us with divine authority and trustworthiness. It not only *contains* the Word of God, but it *is* the Word of God.[8]

5. *Divine rule of practice:* We say of the Scriptures that "they only constitute the divine rule of Christian faith and practice." Man needs a "divine rule of Christian faith and practice." "Christian faith" refers to our doctrine, or what we believe. For instance, man needs to know that he is a fallen creature, a sinner by nature, and by choice. He needs to know that there is a supreme God who created him, loves him, redeemed him through His Son, Jesus, and has planned a glorious eternity for him. This is "Christian faith." These facts God reveals to man in His Word.[9]

"Christian practice" refers to our manner of life and our concept of what is right and wrong. This is called "Christian ethics." We base our conduct upon the Word of God.

During World War II, a worldly-wise American soldier on one of the South Sea Islands saw an islander reading the Bible. With some scorn and superiority the American said to him, "Do you bother with that book over here? We let that go long ago." The islander replied, "Well, maybe you have outgrown the Bible in America, but you ought to be thankful that it got here. If it had not been here before you came, you would already have been boiled alive and eaten!" Yes, man needs guidance for his conscience. That guidance is found in the Bible. It was the Bible that made the South Sea islanders aware of the fact that they should not kill and eat one another. It is the Bible that tells us that we should not steal, hate, live immorally, be greedy, be unkind or quarrel.[10.]

In Summary (Students)

a. The term *"Scripture"* or *"Scriptures"* means *writing*, and always refers to the Bible.[1]

b. "The Old and New Testaments" mean the old and new covenants which God made with man.[2,3a]

c. The old covenant promised a redeemer; the new covenant presented Him.[3b,4]

d. The Old Testament was written in Hebrew; the New in Greek.[5]

e. Inspiration speaks of God working, both through the writers and through the contents of the Bible, to assure the reliability of the Scriptures.[6,7,8]

f. The Bible tells us what to believe. The Bible tells us how to live. We call this a "divine rule of Christian faith and practice."[9,10]

QUESTIONS TO THINK ABOUT

1. What do you think would happen to Christianity if the Bible were suddenly taken away? What would we lose? What would we do?

2. What important relationship is there between a divine rule of faith and a divine rule of practice?

3. Have you read the Bible all the way through? If not, why not?

STUDENTS' REVIEW
LESSON 2

1. The Scriptures have various titles. Match up the following (note that the review material is based on the *New International Version* of the Bible):

   (E) "The word of God"   a. Psalm 119:145
   (F) "The word of the Lord"   b. Galatians 3:10
   (C) "Your statutes"   c. Psalm 119:167
   (A) "Your decrees"   ⌄ d. Matthew 22.40
   (B) "The book of the law"   e. Luke 8:11
   (D) "The law and the prophets" f. 1 Peter 1:25

2. We have observed that the Old Testament is based on the "old covenant," and the New Testament on the "new covenant." By circling the correct answers below, indicate which of the following texts refer to the "old" and which to the "new" covenant.

   Hebrews 8:9   (old) or new
   Jeremiah 31:31   old or (new)
   Jeremiah 31:32   (old) or new
   Hebrews 12:24   old or (new)
   Matthew 26:28   old or (new)
   2 Kings 23:2   (old) or new

3. Remembering what "inspiration" means, choose from the following references those which support the inspiration of the Scriptures. Underline those you choose:

   2 Peter 1:21   Psalm 119:89   Ezekiel 1:3   John 3:16
              Mark 14:38   2 Timothy 3:16,17

4. Since the Bible is the only divine rule of Christian faith or doctrine, choose from among the following Scriptures those which guide us in our *faith* or *doctrine:*

   John 3:16   Romans 3:23   Pslam 139:23,24
           Romans 10:13   Isaiah 12:2,3

5. The Bible is also our divine rule of Christian practice. Choose from among the following those texts which tell us *how to live as Christians:*

   Matthew 6:33   John 9:1   Exodus 20:15
        1 Corinthians 6:20   Ephesians 2:8

8

LESSON 3

IN THE BEGINNING—GOD

The disciple Philip eagerly said to Jesus one day: *"Lord, show us the Father and that will be enough for us"* (John 14:8). Don't we all feel the same? Who is God? What is He like? Does He really care for me? How may I please Him with my life? Does He have a purpose for my life? It is with some of these questions in mind that we begin our study of the second and third doctrines.

OUR SECOND DOCTRINE

Doctrines two and three help us to understand the *being* and *attributes* of God. They tell us these things about Him: He is of infinite perfection in power and glory; He is the Creator, Preserver, and Governor of all; He alone is to be regarded and treated as God (the only proper object of religious worship"; He is one, yet three in one. Let us look now at our second doctrine:

> *We believe there is only one God, who is infinitely perfect, the Creator, Preserver and Governor of all things, and who is the only proper object of religious worship.*

It is true that with our human minds we cannot fully know the infinite God, but it has pleased Him to reveal Himself to us to the limit of our understanding. This revelation has to be expressed in human terms, and these are not wholly sufficient for the task. What we must remember, above all, is that God wants us to know Him, and to that end He revealed Himself through Jesus Christ, the Son.

1. *There is only one God*—Reasons for believing that there is a God are fourfold (and there *are* some atheists, you know):

   a. *Nature.* Just as we know that a house and a watch had to have a maker so the universe must have had a great and wonderful maker. We call Him God.

   b. *Man's inward feelings or intuition.* From time to time we instinctively depend on a superior being; our consciences tell us that there is one greater than we are. We call Him God.

   c. *The Bible.* From the first verse, "in the beginning," to the end of the Bible, "the grace of the Lord Jesus be with God's people," God is revealed.

   d. *The experience of God's people.* We who know His forgiveness, who have been delivered from our sins, and who consciously find the presence of God in our lives probably provide the most convincing of all proofs.[1]

We see, then, that "only *one* God" is declared by the Scriptures from Genesis to Revelation. *"In the beginning God"* (Genesis 1:1) is the very beginning of the Bible, while *"the grace of our Lord Jesus Christ" is the conclusion. The words "From the very beginning the Word was with God"* (John 1:2, *GNB)* witness to *one* God. In the midst of idol-worshiping nations, Abraham recognized that one God ruled the world: *"Will not the judge of all the earth do right?"* (Genesis 18:25). Moses, David, Solomon, Isaiah, then Jesus, Paul, and others all endorse, through the centuries, that "there is only one God." As for the Jew (Deuteronomy 4:39; 6:4), so for the Christian (1 Corinthians 8:4-6 there is "no God but one" (1 Corinthians 8:4).[2]

2. *God is infinitely perfect.* God is perfect in His divine attributes or characteristics. He is "infinitely" perfect in a way that our limited minds cannot fully understand, just as we sometimes find it hard to understand cube root, or Shakespeare, or space flight. Yet the Bible gives us some idea of God's perfect attributes. Our *Handbook of Doctrine* lists eleven: God is personal, spirit, eternal, unchanging, the only God, triune, present everywhere (omnipresent), knows all things (omniscient), is all powerful (omnipotent), has perfect holiness, is perfect love.[3]

3. *God is the Creator of all things.* How did this world and the universe originate? Where did animals and birds and fish come from? And how about man? That indeed is an important question, about which man has formed many plausible and sometimes attractive theories. There are those who suggest that lower forms of life appeared on the planet when some highly favorable conditions prevailed—possibly on a tropical seashore or in a jungle—from which all life evolved to higher levels, finally producing man who is recognized as the most advanced of all creatures. The variations of this theory are numerous, complex, and changing.

Now let us, who are Bible-believing Salvationists, recognize that God can work in any way He desires. Furthermore, He doesn't tell us all the details of how He works. But there are a few things He does tell us in His Word. Let us, then, find a few basic facts from the Word.

The first chapter of Genesis speaks of God the Creator. The key words in this account are *"God created."* "Create" is from the Hebrew word *bara,* which simply means to bring something into existence, something which had not existed before. It is used three important times in Genesis 1, in the first, the 21st, and the 27th verses. Whatever else this may imply, it establishes God as the CREATOR:

    a . the Creator of "the heaven and the earth,"

    b . the Creator of animal life: "every living and moving thing,"

    c . the Creator of man "in His own image."

So the Bible declares that in three different spheres God brought something new into existence—and thus became "the Creator of all living things." We believe this because the Bible says so. See Revelation 4:11.

This answers, for the Bible-believing Christian, the three unanswered and pressing questions of naturalistic evolution with an amazingly simple and satisfying answer:

10

a. The question of *first origin*—"In the beginning GOD CREATED." Except for admitting this simple statement there is an unsolved mystery as to how matter, the universe, and the world originated, for science offers no answer.

b. The question of *beginning of animal* or "sentient" life (life capable of sensation and consciousness): *"And GOD CREATED . . . every living and moving thing."* No real bridge has ever been found from plant life up to animal or sentient life.

c. The question of the *origin of man* upon this earth. *"So God CREATED man in His own image, in the image of God He created him."* There has long been, and will long be, a search for the "missing link" to connect animals to man in an evolutionary ladder. Most important of all, the Bible says that man, as a creature in the image and likeness of God, was a special creation. In a unique sense he, and he alone, was created with some of the attributes of God, with true godliness and enjoying a warm, personal fellowship with his God. This is important![4]

4. *As Preserver and Governor of all things* God rules over that which He has created. He rules over nature. Paul states: *"He is before all things, and in Him all things hold together"* (Colossians 1:17). Scientists proclaim that there is a hidden force which "holds together" in a mysterious fashion, matter, the world, the universe. The Bible reveals that this hidden force is centered in God. As Preserver and Governor, God also rules over men, giving them wise and holy laws for their conduct and their physical well-being, rewarding or punishing them, and overruling all events for the fulfillment of His great purpose. *"The God who made the world and everything in it is the Lord of heaven and earth . . . For in Him we live and move and have our being"* (Acts 17:24,28).[5]

5. *God is the only proper object of religious worship.* Our Lord quoted from the Old Testament, as a rule of mankind: *"Worship the Lord your God, and serve Him only"* (Matthew 4:10). Although more than 90% of all Americans admit the existence of God, they don't all worship Him. Man can truly worship God only when he surrenders himself to God. For example, if you sit in a meeting with wickedness, or hatred, in your heart and mind, you cannot really worship God. The meeting is without meaning, and you are not blessed—until you make things right with God.[6.]

OUR THIRD DOCTRINE *(The Divine Partnership)*

There may be in your town a law firm which carries the names of three persons, for example: ROBINSON, SMITH AND CARUTHERS, or some other combination of names. This means that these people are in partnership together in a law firm. Listing the names in this way is common practice and easily understood. In our *third* doctrine, the divine partnership is expressed in this way:

> *We believe that there are three persons in the*
> *Godhead—the Father, the Son and the Holy Ghost, un-*
> *divided in essence and co-equal in power and glory.*

The following emphases on this doctrine should help you to understand it more clearly.

1. *There are three persons in the Godhead.* This statement is undeniably mysterious, although it is not unlike the law firm where there are three partners in the company. The three persons in the Godhead are *intimated* (that is, there is some reference to the Three) in the Old Testament in such passages as *"Then God said, 'Let us make man in our image' "* (Genesis 1:26) and again *"And now the Sovereign Lord (the Father) has sent Me* (the Son), *with His Spirit* (the Holy Spirit)" (Isaiah 48:16).

The New Testament is more explicit. At our Lord's baptism (Matthew 3:16, 17), Jesus saw the Spirit of God like a dove and heard the voice of His Father say, *"This is My Son, whom I love."* Then the apostolic benediction of 2 Corinthians 13:14 states: *"May the grace of the Lord Jesus Christ, and the Love of God, and the fellowship of the Holy Spirit be with you all."* Thus the Bible establishes that "there are three persons in the Godhead." Sometimes the third person is known as the "Holy Ghost," since "ghost" was an old English term for "spirit." The following may prove helpful:

NOTE, then, that:
> The Father is GOD
> The Son is GOD
> The Holy Spirit is GOD

So that we may properly say:
> God, the Father
> God, the Son
> God, the Holy Spirit

NOTE, however, that the divine *persons* are distinct and separate:
> The FATHER is not the Son, nor the Holy Spirit.
> The SON is not the Holy Spirit, nor the Father.
> The HOLY SPIRIT is not the Father, nor the Son.

"There *are* three persons in the Godhead."
> Although mysterious, the Trinity is an essential doctrine of the Christian Church. God the Father sent His Son into the world to redeem us, and God the Holy Spirit applies the redemptive work to our souls. This we shall see more clearly later.

2. *Undivided in essence and co-equal in power and glory.* The "essence" which binds them together in one is their common nature of deity, of being GOD. (In the law firm they were all lawyers.) The *Father* is God, the *Son* is God, the *Holy Spirit* is God. Their common Godhood, or deity, unites them.

"Co-equal in power and glory" simply recognizes that none is less important or subordinate to another (as though there were no senior partners in the law firm). This is seen in the fact that we are to pray to each divine person. You have often prayed to your heavenly Father; you have often prayed to Jesus. You may also pray to the Holy Spirit. Many of our songs and choruses are prayers to the Holy Spirit, such as "Spirit of the living God . . . " and "Come, thou everlasting Spirit." So each person in the Godhead may be the object of worship, of fellowship, of love.

Imperfect illustrations of the Trinity have been made by reference to a three-leaf clover; to water as liquid, steam, ice; to the three dimensions of space. But these are all faint and inadequate.[7]

3. *Each person in the Trinity is really and truly God.* Since this is so, each is to be treated as God. The first person in the Godhead is especially the Father. He is designated the Father of Jesus Christ in 2 John 3. He is identified in Ephesians 4:6 as *"one God and Father of all, who is over all and through all and in all."* In a particular sense He is the Father of true believers to whom He has given spiritual life. See 2 Corinthians 6:17,18.

In the next lesson we shall discuss the second person in the Trinity.

4. *The Holy Spirit is the third person in the Trinity.* The Holy Spirit is too often neglected. But He is as real as the other two Persons, and shares the divine attributes and works. He was not too well known in Old Testament times. However, He was valued by the Old Testament saints. David cried out to God: *"Do not cast me from Your presence or take Your Holy Spirit from me"* (Psalm 51:11). The Holy Spirit inspired the writers of the Old Testament: *"For no prophetic message ever came just from the will of man, but men were under the control of the Holy Spirit as they spoke the message that came from God"* (2 Peter 1:21, *GNB).*

In the New Testament, He was prominent in the life and work of Jesus: at His incarnation (Luke 1:35); at His baptism when He came like a dove (Luke 3:22); in the promise of Jesus that the Holy Spirit would come in a new way to believers (John 4:16,17).

The Holy Spirit is the helper of men in their spiritual lives (He is sometimes called the "Helper"—(John 14:16,26; 16:7, *GNB):*

    a. He convicts of sin. When speaking about the Holy Spirit Jesus said, *"When He comes, He will convict the world of guilt in regard to sin and righteousness and judgment"* (John 16:8).

    b. He "regenerates" or brings about the new spiritual birth. *"I tell you the truth, unless a man is born of water and the Spirit, he cannot enter the Kingdom of God"* (John 3:5).

    c. He gives assurance that we are saved: *"The Spirit Himself testifies with our spirit that we are God's children"* (Romans 8:16).

    d. He desires to fill us. *"Be filled with the Spirit"* (Ephesians 5:8).[8]

In Summary (Students)

Statements "a" through "e" relate to doctrine two.

a. While most heathen countries believe in many gods, we believe there is only one God.[1,2]

b. Our God has several attributes: He is eternal, unchanging, present everywhere, all-wise and all-powerful. He is also perfect in holiness, in faithfulness, in mercy, and in love.[3]

c. God created the world, the planets, indeed all the universe. He also created man in His own image.[4]

d. God rules in nature and in the hearts of men.[5]

e. We worship God because He loves us and we love Him. We should not worship anyone else, or anything else.[6]

Statements "f" through "i" relate to doctrine three.

f. God the Father, God the Son, and God the Holy Spirit are all divine persons. Therefore, there are three persons in the Godhead.

g. Each is not "a" God, making three Gods. But each is God—in essence or nature. Each is divine. Thus we have one God, but three pesrons, like ice, water and steam which are three forms of H_2O containing the same elements of two parts hydrogen and one part oxygen.[7,8]

h. The first person of the Godhead is known as the Father, the second as the Son, the third as the Holy Spirit or Holy Ghost.

i. The Holy Spirit is "the Helper" in our spiritual experience. He brings conviction of sin; He enables us to be "born again." He assures us of being saved. He is ready to fill our hearts.

QUESTIONS TO THINK ABOUT

Questions one through three relate to doctrine two.

1. In what ways do the gods of heathen countries differ from our God?

2. How does the kind of god and his characteristics or attributes affect the persons who worship that god—whether in a heathen land or in America?

3. Which song in the "Communion with God" section of the *Song Book* do you think best expresses *religious worship?*

Questions four through six relate to doctrine three.

4. What godly characteristics can you think of which might be common to all three persons of the Godhead. You might begin with: being kind, being holy, etc.

5. Find a song in the *Song Book* which speaks of the Trinity. Perhaps you could suggest singing it at this time in the class, or in the meeting this week. What does it say about each person in the Trinity?

6. Is God living? How do you know?

STUDENTS' REVIEW
LESSON 3

The Bible says many things about God. Opposite the text write the one thing which you feel this text says about God. For example: Psalm 19:1 might be either "God's glory" or "His handiwork."

Psalm 90:2 _____

Leviticus 19:2 _____

John 4:24 _____

2 Corinthians 6:17,18 _____

Malachi 3:6 _____

1 John 4:8 _____

Hebrews 4:13 _____

Psalm 86:5 _____

Nehemiah 9:6 _____

Psalm 96:9 _____

2 Corinthians 13:14 _____

Isaiah 64:8 _____

Mark 1:11 _____

Luke 11:13 _____

LESSON 4

JESUS OUR LORD

We have considered the fact that each of the three persons in the Godhead is divine; each is God. But now we will examine that which is *unique* abut Jesus—Jesus as we know Him here on earth. He was not only God—and He *was* God from all eternity—but He also *became* man. That made Him different from the other persons in the Godhead. The heavenly Father never became man. The Holy Spirit never bcame man. Only Jesus did that. That made Him different from other *men*. No man is God, or ever will be. Jesus *is* unique. Our fourth doctrine expresses this truth as follows:

> *We believe that in the person of Jesus Christ the Divine and human natures are united, so that He is truly and properly God and truly and properly man.*

A. JESUS—UNIQUE IN HIS HUMANITY

Everyone you and I know is just plain human. We live in a town or city of men, women, and children. We go to school, or to work, with people who are boys and girls, men and women. Not one, not even the most godly person we may know, would claim that he/she is God. But Jesus is both man *and* God.

1. *"We believe that in the person of Jesus Christ the Divine and human natures are united."* It was through His marvelous birth at Bethlehem that Jesus, in a mystical and unique way, became man as well as God. Through Mary, His earthly mother, He took upon Himself our human nature. Yet, because He had no earthly father, but came into being through the Holy Spirit, He continued to be God. Thus He became both God and man. Paul declared (Philippians 2:5-7): *"Christ Jesus . . . being in very nature God . . . made Himself nothing, taking the very nature of a servant . . . being found in appearance as a man."* Jesus was born like a man; He appeared in human likeness. This union of God with man, or the clothing of the divine person with human nature, is called "the incarnation." The dictionary defines it as "the union of divinity with humanity in Christ."[1]

It was needful for Jesus Christ to be *both* God and man in order to accomplish our redemption. As *man* He suffered on man's behalf, and fully understands man's temptations and sorrows. As *God* He atoned for our sins and thus procured our salvation. We shall study that more fully in another lesson. God did not remain in heaven and study man from a distance; but through Jesus Christ, His Son, He actually became man. So, because He is now both man and God, He can supply divine help and comfort to us. Hebrews 2:18 states: *"Because He Himself suffered when He was tempted, He is able to help those who are being tempted."* And Peter (1 Peter 5:7) urges: *"Cast all your anxiety on Him because He cares for you."* What an encouragement that is to us!

16

B. JESUS—TRULY AND PROPERLY GOD

Our fourth doctrine states, "We believe that in the person of Jesus Christ, the Divine and human natures are united, so that He is TRULY AND PROPERLY GOD and TRULY AND PROPERLY MAN." That He is truly and properly *God* is established by:

1. *His pre-existence as God from all eternity.* Calling Jesus "the Word," John records (1:1): *"In the beginning was the Word, and the Word was with God, and the Word was God."* And John the Baptist, older than Jesus by several months, said of Him in that first century (1 John 1:15): *"This was He of whom I said, 'He who comes after me has surpassed me because He was before me.' "* And Jesus spoke to His father about *"the glory I had with You before the world began"* (John 17:5). We see, then, that Jesus had lived as God from the beginning.

2. *His divine names and titles.* These indicate that "He is truly and properly God": *"The Word was with God and the Word was God* (John 1:1). Paul cried out: *" . . . Our great God and Saviour, Jesus Christ"* (Titus 2:13).

3. *His divine attributes, which can only belong to God.* These include:

a. Eternal Existence: *"He was with God in the beginning"* (John 1:2).

b. Omnipotence: *"Jesus came to them and said, 'All authority in heaven and on earth has been given to Me"* (Matthew 28:18).

c. Omnipresence: *"For where two or three come together in My name, there am I with them"* (Matthew 18:20).

d. Omniscience: *"Christ, in whom are hidden all the treasures of wisdom and knowledge"* (Colossians 2:2,3).

No *man* can acquire these attributes. They belong only to God.

4. *His divine works which also speak of His divinity.*

a. Creation: *"Through Him all things were made; without Him nothing was made that has been made"* (John 1:3).

b. Forgiveness of sins: *"That ye may know that the Son of Man has authority on earth to forgive sins"* (Mark 2:10).

c. Raising of the dead: (John 5:28,29; John 11:38-44).

5. *His acceptance of worship:* This shows that He claimed to be God. *"Then they worshiped Him and returned to Jerusalem with great joy"* (Luke 24:52).[2]

C. JESUS—TRULY AND PROPERLY MAN

How do we know that "He is truly and properly man?" We have the evidence from God's Word. Let us examine it:

1. The Bible says so: *"Jesus of Nazareth was a man accredited by God to you by miracles, wonders, and signs . . . "* (Acts 2:22).

2. He possessed a human *body.* He hungered, ate, thirsted, was weary, slept, wept, and died.[3]

3. He possessed a human *soul* and a human *spirit.* In Gethsemane

He said, *"My soul is overwhelmed with sorrow to the point of death"* (Matthew 26:38). And on the cross He prayed, *"Father, into Your hands I commit My spirit"* (Luke 23:46).

4. He was very human in His many *temptations.* *" . . . We have one who has been tempted in every way, just as we are—yet was without sin"* (Hebrews 4:15).[4]

D. *JESUS—STILL 'TRULY AND PROPERLY GOD' AND 'TRULY AND PROPERLY MAN'*

Jesus is *still* "truly and properly God and truly and properly man," even in heaven. This may be a great surprise, but it is also a great comfort to us. For He *still* understands us, and can help us. After the crucifixion, speaking of Jesus as our high priest, the writer of Hebrews said: *"Therefore, since we have a great high priest who has gone through the heavens, Jesus the Son of God, let us hold firmly to the faith we profess. For we do not have a high priest who is unable to sympathize with our weaknesses, but we have one who has been tempted in every way, just as we are—yet was without sin. Let us then approach the throne of grace with confidence, so that we may receive mercy and find grace to help us in our time of need"* (Hebrews 4:14-16). Long after Jesus left this earth Paul wrote: *"For there is one God and one mediator between God and men, the man Christ Jesus"* (1 Timothy 2:5).[5]

In Summary (Students)

a. Jesus is both man and God. He is the only one who ever was both man and God. He is God-man.[1]

b. We know that He is God because He has lived from all eternity, because He has names and titles given only to God, because He has divine attributes and characteristics: *omnipotence* (all-powerful), *omnipresence* (present everywhere), *omniscience* (infinite knowledge); because He did what only God can do, such as *create, forgive sins, raise the dead.* And when people *worshiped Him,* He did not forbid then, but accepted the worship.[2]

c. He was human. The Gospels prove this. He acted like a man in every way. He was tempted like a man. He is still man in heaven.

d. As man He understands us; He can help us when we are tempted. As man He suffered for us.[3,4]

e. As God He died for our sins. As God He can help us to live victorious over sin.[5]

QUESTIONS TO THINK ABOUT

1. Explain in your own words what is meant by the incarnation.

2. What do you think were God's reasons for wanting Jesus here on earth in human form?

3. Do you think that Jesus was tempted again after His great temptation in the widlerness? Give reasons for your answer.

4. Why do you think God wanted Jesus here with a divine nature?

5. Are your temptations like those of Jesus? How can He help you?

STUDENTS' REVIEW
LESSON 4

From the Scripture references listed below find supporting texts for each of the following:

1. We believe that in the person of Jesus Christ the divine and human natures are united: _____

_____

2. We believe that Jesus is truly God: _____

_____

3. We believe that Jesus is truly man: _____

_____

1 John 5:20	Titus 2:13
Philippians 2:5-7	Hebrews 4:15
1 Timothy 2:5	2 Peter 1:1
Romans 1:3,4	Acts 2:22
John 1:14	1 Timothy 3:16

LESSON 5

MAN'S SIN—GOD'S REMEDY

We know that God loves us and provides and cares for His children. Why is it then that so many disobey Him and fall into sin and wrongdoing? Why do people sin?

Sometimes because they do not know. Sometimes people do what God does not want them to do because they simply do not know His will. They are ignorant of His laws. They have not heard His Word. They live in darkness. They are less to be blamed and more to be taught.

Sometimes because they make mistakes. Everybody makes mistakes at times. They may be mistaken in judgment, or lacking in maturity. A child who wants to help her father weed the garden may pull up the flowers with the weeds because they look alike. A father gives his son a football for a birthday present, but the boy would much rather have had a pair of skates; the father was mistaken about what his son really wanted. Sometimes a person plays a joke on another "just for fun," but really hurts the feelings of his friend, who does not "see the joke." It turns out to be an unhappy mistake.

We usually learn by our mistakes. We may be chagrined, we may feel very sorry, but we do not need to feel guilty. And when our friends make mistakes, we should not condemn them but try to help them. As Paul puts it: *"Brothers, if someone is caught in a sin, you who are spiritual should restore him gently. But watch yourself, or you also may be tempted. Carry each other's burdens, and in this way you will fulfill the law of Christ"* (Galatians 6:1,2).

We know that people sometimes *choose* to do wrong. Our fifth doctrine states this truth clearly, and because disobedience to God rightly exposes the sinner to the wrath of God, He provided an atonement for man's disobedience and sin. Our sixth doctrine states this truth about the atonement, and we are going to study these two doctrines in this lesson.

OUR FIFTH DOCTRINE

When people choose to do wrong they sin, for they know that they are disobedient to God. This may be because they want to do what *they* want to do. Sin is basically selfish. A child willfully plays after school when she knows her mother expects her to come right home to practice the piano. A wife willfully nags her husband, although she knows he is tired after a day's hard work. A person willfully lies, steals, or covets that which belongs to his friends.

Sometimes a person sins because it is the easier way. If he does what is right, his friends will taunt him and laugh at him. He doesn't want to be different from his peers.

Sometimes a person sins by not doing what he knows he should do. Jesus gave the example of the "good Samaritan" who helped the

21

injured Jew. The other two men had *avoided* helping the wounded stranger. They left undone the good they should have done.

But people sin chiefly because we all are born of a sinful race. That is the basic reason for it all. Our fifth doctrine states this truth clearly:

> *We believe that our first parents were created in a state of innocency, but by their disobedience they lost their purity and happiness, and that in consequence of their fall all men have become sinners, totally depraved, and as such are justly exposed to the wrath of God.*

1. *This starts with primitive history. We believe that our first parents were created in a state of innocency.* In considering the second doctrine it was observed that man, created in the image and likeness of God (Genesis 1:27), was a *special* creation. In a unique sense he, and he alone, was created with some of the attributes of God—with true godliness, and with a warm, personal fellowship with God. Not the animals, nor the fish, nor the birds of the air; only man could walk and talk with God.[1]

In this Godlikeness, in this fellowship with God, Adam and Eve were in "a state of innocency." That is, they were free from guilt, as they were free from sin. They were of a pure heart, as God is pure, as God is free from sin.

But by their disobedience they lost their purity and happiness. God tested our first parents by a single plain command, and warned them that death would be the consequence of disobedience: *"You are free to eat from any tree in the garden; but you must not eat from the tree of knowledge of good and evil, for when you eat of it you will surely die"* (Genesis 2:16,17).

As recorded in Genesis 3, temptation came from the devil, or Satan, who appeared in the form of a serpent. The temptation was threefold:

    a. Satan suggested *doubt* concerning God's goodness. *"Did God really say, 'You must not eat from any tree in the garden'?"* (Genesis 3:1).

    b. He encouraged *disbelief* in God's warning by saying brazenly: "You will not surely die" (v.4).

    c. He stirred up *desire* for what God had forbidden: *"For God knows that when you eat of it your eyes will be opened, and you will be like God, knowing good and evil"* (v.5).

2. Thus SIN BEGAN AMONG MANKIND when our first parents, Adam and Eve, yielding to the devil's temptation, disobeyed God's righteous command (v.6). This is called "the fall." In this account there are four persons. God is clearly identified as "the Lord God." In Revelation 12:9 and 20:2, Satan is identified as the "old" or "ancient" serpent of the Genesis account. And Adam, in the pages of sacred history, is identified as one individual, a person as real as you and I, as real as Jesus who is termed "the last Adam" and "the second Adam"

in 1 Corinthians 15:45 and 47: *"So it is written: 'The first man Adam became a living being'; the last Adam, a life-giving spirit . . . The first man was of the dust of the earth, the second man from heaven."* Obviously, Paul was here speaking of the creation of man. And he speaks of the fall when he compares Adam as the "one man" who brought sin into the world, with Jesus as the "one man" who brought grace and justification into the world: *" . . . Sin entered the world through one man . . . how much more did God's grace and the gift that came by the grace of one man, Jesus Christ, overflow to the many!"* (Romans 5:12,15). Eve is the fourth person identified in the account of the fall.

It is well then to realize that, on a given occasion in history, two real people, Adam and Eve, were tempted by a very real devil, and disobeyed a very real God. This is called *"the fall."*[2]

3. *In consequence of their fall all men have become sinners, totally depraved, and as such are justly exposed to the wrath of God.* Because of their disobedience, not only did Adam and Eve become sinners, but all their children through the centuries have become sinners. Paul declares this in Romans 5:12 and 3:23: *"Therefore, just as sin entered the world through one man, and death through sin, and in this way death came to all men, because all sinned . . . for all have sinned and fall short of the glory of God."* The perfect man of creation was marred when Adam sinned. Since then people have a natural bent, or tendency, to sin. This is called "depravity." And since we are all descendants from our first parents, Adam and Eve, we all have inherited this sin-marred nature—this tendency to sin.[3]

4. *All have become sinners.* We learn from God's Word, then, that *all* have become sinners, totally depraved, and are "justly exposed to the wrath of God."[4]

OUR SIXTH DOCTRINE

We have been talking about man's sinful condition, and now we are to learn what God has done about it all. Since all men have become sinners and are justly exposed to His wrath, what *has* God done about this situation? When, in a community or a city, men break the law they are arrested, tried, and sentenced to jail. But what would happen if *all* men broke the law, and all were guilty of crime? That is the problem which faced our heavenly Father for "all *have* sinned and come short of the glory of God." Will He punish everybody? Or will He just excuse some and not others? Or will He decide that it is not necessary to punish anybody?

As the Christian Church studies the Scriptures it says, with the Army, this truth which is stated in our sixth doctrine:

We believe that the Lord Jesus Christ has by His suffering and death made an atonement for the whole world so that whosoever will may be saved.

1. *Yes, God has done something about it!* "The Lord Jesus Christ has by His suffering and death made an atonement for the whole

world." Now atonement is the redeeming effect of Christ's incarnation (becoming a man), His sufferings (on the cross), and His death. Thus the cross is at the center of the atonement. Put simply, the atonement means that Christ Jesus in His death dealt completely with the problem of sin. So since, through the fall, all of us became sinful, in the atonement Christ assumed the guilt of us all.[5]

2. *Biblical clarity.* Regarding the atonement, there are some truths that the Bible makes very clear and which we can understand:

a. *Love*—The first truth is that the atonement expresses the loving heart of a God who cares. What of John 3:16: *"God so loved the world that He gave . . . "*? Or consider Romans 5:8: *"But God demonstrates His own love for us in this: While we were still sinners, Christ died for us."* God the Father and God the Son are one in their love for us. Paul testifies regarding *"the Son of God who loved me and gave Himself for me"* (Galatians 2:20). And John dedicates *"glory and power forever and ever"* to Jesus who *"loves us and has freed us from our sins by His blood"* (Revelation 1:5).[6]

b. *Sin*—The Bible emphasizes that the sin of man made the atonement necessary. However, Jesus was not forced into an unwilling death. Nor was His death a matter of mere chance. His death was planned in eternity. He died for—because of—our sins (1 Corinthians 15:3). Christ's blood was shed *"for the forgiveness of sins"* (Matthew 26:28).[7]

c. *Substitution*—Christ on the cross took the penalty of our sins. Thus, although we all will have to physically die, like the thief on the cross, we may again live "with Him in paradise." As Jesus died for the thief on the cross, so He died for all of us. His death became the atoning sacrifice. The Old Testament had foreshadowed this in the sacrificing of an animal (usually a lamb) for the sins of the people. When they saw the lamb die they cried out, "He dies in my place." All this pointed forward to the time when Jesus would fulfill that Old Testament type. This is why Paul declared in 1 Corinthians 15:3: *"Christ died for our sins according to the Scriptures."* That is what John meant when, on seeing Jesus, he declared: *"Look, the Lamb of God, who takes away the sin of the world"* (John 1:29).[8]

The substitutionary death of Christ on the cross so that we would not have to die spiritually is taught in many Scriptures. Put "instead of" or "in place of" where we find the word "for" in the following statements: Christ said: *"I am the good shepherd. The good shepherd lays down his life for* (in place of) *the sheep"* (John 10:11). *"Christ died for* (instead of) *the ungodly . . . While we were still sinners, Christ died for us* (in our place)" (Romans 5:6,8). *"And He died for* (in the place of) *all, that those who live should no longer live for themselves, but for Him who died for them and was raised again"* (2 Corinthians 5:15). Yes, He paid the price of our sin and guilt on the tree.

24

The sufferings of no other would have been adequate or sufficient. Since all have sinned, all have merited punishment for their sins; none by his own death can pay the penalty of another. Only one who was under no penalty for His own sin could atone for the sins of mankind. In Revelation the song is directed to Jesus (Revelation 5:9): *"You are worthy ... because You were slain, and with Your blood You purchased men for God from every tribe and language and people and nation."*

> *There was no other good enough*
> *To pay the price of sin;*
> *He only could unlock the gate*
> *Of heaven, and let us in.*

So John points out, *"He is the atoning sacrfice for our sins, and not only for ours but also for the sins of the whole world"* (1 John 2:2).

Atonement then is the *means* by which God brings the *results:* reconciliation and redemption.[9]

3. "The Lord Jesus Christ has by His suffering and death made an atonement for the whole world so that whosoever will may be saved." Two things are expressed here:

a. *Man must exert his "will" to be saved.* Revelation 22:17 expresses it in this way: *" ... Whoever wishes, let him take the free gift of the water of life."* The "whoever won't" will never be saved. Jesus told some unbelievers. *"Yet you refuse to come to Me to have life"* (John 5:40). It is like fresh air and exercise. There is a lot to be had, but it is only the one who is willing to give it time who will keep healthy and well. Like much education, it is free, but only he who is willing to work at it will benefit. Man must be willing, for God will not force any man to accept His gift of salvation.

b. *The atonement is made for the whole world.* God excludes none. There are no favorites. God's door of mercy is open to all. God invites the whole world. He said *whosoever,* and we believe that He means it! It will be helpful to know, too, that "whosoever" is always singular in number. We come in through God's door of mercy, one by one.[10]

In Summary (Students)

Statements "a" through "e" relate to doctrine five.

a. Sin is willful disobedience to the known will of God. Sometimes this is in bad things done; sometimes it is in good things not done.

b. Our first parents, Adam and Eve, were created without sin or guilt before God.[1]

c. Sin entered the human family when our first parents willfully disobeyed God. This is known as "the fall," when "sin came into the world through one man."[2]

d. We have all inherited from our first parents a disposition, or natural tendency, to sin. This is called depravity.[3]

e. Because of our inherited tendency to sin we all have committed sins, and thus need God's saving grace.[4]

Statements "f" through "i" relate to doctrine six.

f. The redeeming effect of Christ's incarnation (becoming a man), His sufferings, and His death on the cross are the components of "the atonement."[5]

g. Three facets or aspects of the atonement are: *Love:* that concern for mankind which impelled God in Christ to make an atonement.[6] *Sin:* the disobedience which produced the need of an atonement.[7] *Substitution:* It was Jesus who paid the death penalty for sin "in place of" the sinner.[8,9]

h. Man's *willingness* to be saved is necesssary for his salvation. God forces no one to accept His gift of salvation.

i. God includes *everyone* in His provision of an atonement and in His invitation to be saved.[10]

QUESTIONS TO THINK ABOUT

Questions one through four relate to doctrine five.

1. Who or what determines whether the wrong things we do are done in ignorance, are mistakes of judgment, or are done willfully?

2. Should we feel guilty about our mistakes? What about regret?

3. What should we learn from our mistakes?

4. Why have "all men" become sinners? Is it not possible that some good people have stayed righteous? Have never committed a sin? Don't need to be saved?

Questions five through 10 relate to doctrine six.

5. Some people do not accept the divinity of Christ. What effect would that have on the atonement?

6. Why do you think that God makes it necessary for people to "will" or to want to be saved before they can be saved?

7. What could you say to someone who says, "I am too wicked to be saved?"

8. Can you think of some other "whosoever" verses? What are they?

9. What do we really mean when we sing: *"What can wash away my sins? Nothing but the blood of Jesus"? (The Salvation Army Song Book,* No. 231). Or: *"Would you be free from your burden of sin? There's power in the blood"? (Song Book,* No. 1013).

10. What effect has the atonement had on *your* life?

26

STUDENTS' REVIEW
LESSON 5

1. Match up a Scripture verse with each statement.

   ( ) Man was created in the "image" or "likeness" of God.

   ( ) Our first parents lost their purity and happiness through sin.

   ( ) As a consequence of the fall *all* men have become sinners.

   ( ) All men, *as sinners,* are justly exposed to the wrath of God.
   - a. Isaiah 53:6
   - b. Genesis 5:1
   - c. John 3:36
   - d. Genesis 3:8

2. Remembering that the atonement is the redeeming effect of Christ's becoming a man, His sufferings, and His death on the cross, choose from among the following those texts which refer to the atonement. Circle them.

   Romans 5:6
   Matthew 5:44
   1 Peter 1:18,19
   1 John 5:11,12
   Titus 2:13,14

3. Read the verses listed below. In the *King James Version* there is one word which they all have in common. It is _____.

John 3:16,18	John 11:26
Romans 10:13	John 12:46
Revelation 22:17	Matthew 10:32
Luke 6:47	

27

LESSON 6

WHAT CAN WE DO ABOUT SIN?

There are many things we may not understand in God's plan of salvation for us. But one thing is plain: God wants to forgive our sins. He did His part at Calvary; He is ready to do His part now. But there is something we must do. For example, education is provided by the community, but we have to do our part to become educated. In Lesson Five we learned that man's part is to *will* to be saved. Now the question is: "What must *we* be willing to do?" As Salvationists, we declare in our seventh doctrine:

> We believe that repentance towards God, faith in our Lord Jesus Christ, and regeneration by the Holy Spirit, are necessary to salvation.

The Army always has been and always will be immediately associated with salvation, for we are *The Salvation Army.* We believe that all men may be and should be saved. This is our message in every aspect of our operations. This decisive act of becoming saved is sometimes called conversion, sometimes a commitment to Christ, sometimes a decision for Christ, and sometimes saying a big "Yes" to God. But, whatever it is called, every person must make his own decision. In the Army, the decision is often associated with coming to the penitent-form. But we must realize that coming to the altar in a meeting does not save us. Its value is in the decision it indicates, in the opportunity for prayer, and for counseling which it affords. It is a public witness that we want to be saved, but this public act of itself does not save us. Neither is it necessary to come to the penitent-form in a public meeting in order to be saved. Many are saved in other places and other ways. It must be remembered, however, that Christ said that a public confession on our part will merit a public confession in heaven that we are His.

1. *Conditions necessary to salvation.* There are conditions which are necessary to salvation and two of them are *repentance* and *faith.* This is scriptural. *"You know that I have not hesitated to preach anything that would be helpful to you but have taught you publicly and from house to house ... repentance and ... faith in our Lord Jesus,"* Paul declared to the elders of the church at Ephesus (Acts 20:20,21).[1,2]

2. *Repentance toward God is necessary to salvation.* Now repentance comes from and includes deep sorrow for sin. The psalmist (38:18) said, *"I am troubled by my sin."* Paul declared (2 Corinthians 7:10): *"Godly sorrow brings repentance that leads to salvation ... "* *"Then Peter remembered the words Jesus had spoken: 'Before the rooster crows, you will disown Me three times.' And he went outside and wept bitterly"* (Matthew 26:75).

This aspect of repentance is sometimes called *"contrition."* It is genuine sorrow for sin. But this is *not* just being sorry for *being caught,* or mere regret for the consequences of sin apart from forsaking it. Rather, it is being sorry because we have grieved God.[3]

But the word *repentance means basically a change of attitude*—a change of mind, a change of purpose, a change of action. A person may think that poison ivy is very attractive and plan to plant it in his garden, until he learns the truth about it. Then he would change his attitude toward it and change his plan for using it. Thus the sinner who has clung to sin and resisted the Holy Spirit, upon repenting, changes his mind, his attitude, and determines, by the help of God, to do just the opposite.[4]

Repentance stems from a conviction of sin. The penitent reconizges that he is guilty and deserving of punishment. The brothers of Joseph cried out in a sense of guilt regarding their treatment of Joseph: *"Surely we are being punished because of our brother . . . that's why this distress has come upon us"* (Genesis 42:21).

There are both divine and human elements in repentance. God the Holy Spirit convicts of sin: *"When He* (the Holy Spirit) *comes, He will convict the world of guilt in regard to sin and righteousness and judgment"* (John 16:8). Hence the Scripture declares that repentance is given by God: *". . . God's kindness leads you toward repentance"* (Romans 2:4). Also see Acts 5:31. At the same time there is the human element: *". . . Now He commands all people everywhere to repent. For He has set a day when He will judge the world"* (Acts 17:30,31). God "leads" men to repentance, offers repentance, but man must respond. He is a creature of free will. You may *know* that you should apologize to your friend for being mean to him/her, but you have a terrible battle with yourself to really do it. Your conscience bothers you, but *you* are the one who must make the apology.

3. *This repentance is toward God* (Acts 20:21) *because all sin is primarily against God.* Sin is a transgression of God's law; it is a battle of man's will against God's will. David cried out in the agony of his guilt: *"Against You, You only, have I sinned and done what is evil in your sight"* (Psalm 51:4).[6]

4. *Faith in our Lord Jesus Christ* (Acts 20:21) *is the second condition of salvation.* This truth is clearly stated in the well-known John 3:16. Let us examine it: *"Whoever believes in Him."* This is saving faith—faith, or confidence, that Christ's death is a sufficient payment, sacrifice, atonement for all our sins. There is nothing more that we can add in the way of being good or doing good in order that we might be saved. This is why we sing: *"Just as I am, without one plea, but that Thy blood was shed for me"* and *"We have no other argument, we want no other plea; it is enough that Jesus died, and that He died for me."*

Furthermore, saving faith is an act of entrustment, or surrender. Faith means trust. To believe means to entrust, to commit. The Greek word "believe" is translated "entrust" in John 2:24: *"Jesus would not entrust Himself to them."* To entrust oneself to another is to surrender, to commit. In John 3:16, we are encouraged to surrender, to entrust, to commit ourselves into the care of Jesus, into His will, into His pattern of life. It might well be translated: *"... Whoever commits himself to Him shall not perish ..."* That's saving faith, sometimes called "heart faith." See Romans 10:9-11.[7]

We are willing to commit ourselves to Christ because God really cares, because He has provided a plan of salvation which we know as the atonement: *"For God so loved the world that He gave His one and only Son."*

This faith that saves is not faith in the Church, nor in men or leaders, not even in the Scriptures, but in the divine Person which these Scriptures reveal—*faith in our Lord Jesus Christ.*[8]

5. *Regeneration by the Holy Spirit.* If repentance and faith are things *we* must express, regeneration is "by the Holy Spirit"; it is what *God* does. It is one aspect of the redemption made possible by the atonement. The word "regeneration" really means a new start, a spiritual rebirth. It does not mean that we can, or should, become babies again, but that He will start us over again spiritually. When talking to Nicodemus, Jesus called it being "born again" (John 3:7). Then He explained that it was not a physical, but a spiritual, birth to which He was referring—being "born of the Spirit." Jesus also described it as a spiritual resurrection: *"Whoever hears My words and believes ... he has crossed over from death to life"* (John 5:24). Paul termed it becoming "a new creation" (2 Corinthians 5:17).[9]

This regeneration is *by the Holy Spirit.* When speaking to Nicodemus about the new birth, Jesus said: *"Flesh gives birth to flesh, but the Spirit gives birth to spirit"* (John 3:6).[10]

In Summary (Students)

a. *Repentance* and *faith* are necessary on our part to be saved.[1,2]

b. Repentance includes not only being *sorry* for sin, but also a new or changed *attitude* toward sin.[3,4,5]

c. Since sin is against God, repentance must be toward God.[6]

d. Faith includes a confidence in the atonement or sacrificial death of Jesus. It also includes a surrender to God for everything.[7,8]

e. Regeneration means starting over. Jesus described it when He called it being spiritually born again, and when He used the idea of a spiritual resurrection from death to life.[9]

f. Regeneration is God's part of our being saved. The Holy Spirit is the one who carries this out.[10]

QUESTIONS TO THINK ABOUT

1. If a person is caught "shoplifting," what will he or she have to do in order to show true repentance?

2. Why do you think God requires repentance for salvation?

3. What would you say to a person who emphasizes that to be saved you need "only believe?"

4. Explain your experience of being "born again."

5. Read the seventh doctrine again and see if you can find the evidence of the Trinity.

STUDENTS' REVIEW
LESSON 6

The three things that are required for salvation, our seventh doctrine declares, are: (1) *repentance;* (2) *faith* (on our part); (3) *regeneration* (on God's part).

Considering these as (1), (2), and (3), match them with the following Scriptures:

( ) Acts 3:19
( ) Acts 16:31
( ) Titus 3:5
( ) Ephesians 2:8
( ) 1 Peter 1:23
( ) John 3:36
( ) Acts 17:30
( ) Acts 2:38
( ) John 1:12,13

LESSON 7

SAVED, CERTAIN, AND FAITHFUL

In this lesson we will cover studies on our eighth and ninth doctrines. Doctrine eight helps us to understand how we are justified by grace through faith in Jesus Christ, and how we can be certain of this fact. Doctrine nine helps us to understand that being a Christian is more than making a decision to accept Christ into our lives, as important as that is, but it is also a continuing way of life—a way of obedience, of faithfulness.

OUR EIGHTH DOCTRINE

If we hurt the feelings of a friend who loves us very much, we will want to be forgiven. And that is just what God wants to do for us, if we will let Him, for He does love us. It is in that spirit that we declare in our eighth doctrine:

*We believe that we are justified by grace through faith
in our Lord Jesus Christ and that he that believeth hath
the witness in himself.*

1. *One of the great blessings of salvation.* Forgiveness of sins is another of the great blessings of salvation. To say that we are justified means especially that "we are forgiven."[1]Forgiveness is also called pardon and remission. In the Bible, you find that all of these terms mean basically the same thing. So, added to regeneration, or becoming a new creation in Christ Jesus, is the wonderful experience of forgiveness. One of the sweetest statements we can hear from a loved one, or from a loving God is: "I forgive you." Peter declared (Acts 5:30,31): *"The God of our fathers raised Jesus from the dead—whom you had killed by hanging Him on a tree. God exalted Him to His own right hand as Prince and Saviour that He might give repentance and forgiveness of sins to Israel."* Was Peter thinking of some precious moment, after that dark night of denial, when Jesus must have said to him, "Peter, I forgive you?"

2. *God's forgiveness is different from man's.* We must note that God does not forgive as man does. Man forgives a person the *penalty* of his wrongdoing. The guilty person then does not have to pay the fine, or go to jail. But God paid the *penalty* in the atonement, the death of Jesus on the cross, and then He forgives that guilty person his sins. This upholds God's law of righteousness by not forfeiting or cancelling the penalty, yet allows Him to forgive or remit the sin.

We must remember that since all sins are against God, He is the only one who can forgive them. He is the only one who can take away our guilt. It is as if you have done something mean to your sister. It will do no good to go to your brother to ask forgiveness—he cannot forgive you; even your mother cannot forgive you. You simply must go to your sister—she is the only one who can forgive you.[2]

3. *Release or forgiveness.* The Greek word translated "forgiveness" and "pardon" and "remission" carries the thought of release or deliverance. God does not leave man in his sins and guilt when He forgives him. The pentinent is *released* from his sins. *". . . And you are to give Him the name Jesus, because He will save His people from their sins"* (Matthew 1:21).[3,4]

4. *"We are justified by grace through faith in our Lord Jesus Christ."* In this dishonest world there are people who will try to *bribe* the judge, or to *buy* their way out of jail. Our God will not be bribed by our good works. We cannot buy our way to heaven by self-righteousness. There's nothing we can *do* to merit His forgiveness. Our penalty is paid, and our sins forgiven simply and only because of the *grace* of God.

Now grace is the undeserved favor of God. It is God's great love in action. It is mercy outpoured. The grace of God has its foundation at Calvary, its power in the atonement. As Paul put it, *"But God demonstrates His own love for us in this: While we were still sinners, Christ died for us"* (Romans 5:8). More than that, grace is God at work. The dictionary rightly declares: "Grace is divine *assistance* given to man for his regeneration (his spiritual rebirth) and his sanctification (his cleansing)." So Paul announces: *"For it is by grace you have been saved, through faith—and this not from yourselves, it is the gift of God—not by works, so that no one can boast"* (Ephesians 2:8,9).[5]

5. *"He that believeth hath the witness in himself."* Taken directly from 1 John 5:10 *(KJV),* this statement tells us that we may know that we are saved. It is something like that quiet, assured feeling when we are safe in the house during a violent blizzard outside. We are sheltered and secure. Every child of God may sing: *"Blessed assurance, Jesus is mine."*

OUR NINTH DOCTRINE

We mentioned at the beginning of this study that being a Christian is a continuing way of life, and that is not always easy. In fact the devil sees to it that it is not easy. God has, however, provided some wonderful means of strength and guidance for us. One of the most important of these is the Bible—His Word. Use it! Learn to rely on it! Love it!

There are other Christians who will help you: your corps officer; a sincere soldier (young or old); possibly your parents; or a husband or wife. Listen to the counsel of the wise, and remember to pray. You have the right and privilege of calling upon God, of enjoying fellowship with Him, and of listening to Him. Do it! And don't forget to attend meetings at the corps. There is no real substitute for the warmth and instruction of a good meeting. You will contribute to the blessing possible through the meeting by your singing, your faith, your testimony and, possibly, with your "Hallelujah!"

In the ninth doctrine we have been given the basic condition of victorious living, together with a grave warning:

We believe that continuance in a state of salvation depends upon continued obedient faith in Christ. (In other words: We believe that the Scriptures teach that not only does continuance in the favor of God depend upon continued faith in, and obedience to, Christ, but that it is possible for those who have been truly converted to fall away and be eternally lost.)

1. *The Christian is saved through faith which includes commitment.* That same faith which was necessary to be saved is also necessary to *keep* saved. It is required that such faith be a continuing commitment—a day-by-day experience. Note that in John 3:16 the word "believes" is in the present tense, a continued process—not just a "once-for-all" act of faith. This is frequently stated in the Bible. Take for example John 5:24: *"I tell you the truth, whoever hears My Word and believes Him who sent Me has eternal life."* In this case both "hear" and "believe" are in the present tense. If you put them into the past tense—"heard," "believed," and you "had" eternal life—you have cancelled the great benefit of eternal life.

The Scriptures agree that continuance in a state of salvation depends upon continued obedient faith in Christ. You wouldn't expect it to be otherwise. It's true everywhere. If you are going to be safe in the jungle, stay with your guide. If you are going to be safe on the highways, obey the traffic laws. If you are going to be safe on the water, don't rock the boat. If you are going to be safe (saved) as a Christian, keep your commitment to your Saviour.[6]

2. *Promises are made to those who remain faithful.* God's Word clearly promises: *"Be faithful, even to the point of death, and I will give you the crown of life"* (Revelation 2:10).[7]

3. *Many grave warnings are pronounced against those who prove unfaithful.* *"If a righteous man turns from his righteousness and commits sin, he will die for it; because of the sin he has committed he will die,"* so it is declared in Ezekiel 18:26. In the New Testament, Hebrews 10:26,27, we are warned: *"If we deliberately keep on sinning after we have received the knowledge of the truth, no sacrifice for sins is left, but only a fearful expectation of judgment and of raging fire that will consume the enemies of God."* You see, it could hardly be otherwise. If the law tells you not to walk against the red light, you are likely to get hurt, or even killed, if you do so. Since the law of gravity tells you not to jump off a five-story building, you are foolish if you do so![8]

There are *examples* in the Bible of backsliders who were once saved, but died in their sins. King Saul is one of the saddest. He received "another heart" and yet tried to kill David. He directed the murder of many priests at Nob, and he died a suicide. It is miserable to be a backslider. Most of us know what it is like. But it is actually terrifying to think of dying while away from God. As warnings are erected to keep people away from high-voltage wires or from thin ice on a pond, so God has erected His warning signs. It is plainly necessary, then, that every child of God should beware of the warning signs, for if he does not, he may fall when he thinks he is standing firm.[9]

4. *Assurance is given that we need not backslide.* Although people may become unfaithful, God is faithful, and *"will not let you be tempted beyond what you can bear. But when you are tempted, He will also provide a way out so that you can stand up under it"* (1 Corinthians 10:13). As Hebrews 10:23 again declares: *"He who promised is faithful."* Then Paul speaks his confidence to Timothy: *"Yet I am not ashamed, because I know whom I have believed, and am convinced that He is able to guard what I have entrusted to Him for that day"* (2 Timothy 1:12).[10]

5. *We have our own responsibilities.* We have the responsibility to *"watch and pray so that you will not fall into temptation"* (Matthew 26:41); the responsibility to *"grow in the grace and knowledge of our Lord and Saviour Jesus Christ"* (2 Peter 3:18); the responsibility to *"do your best to present yourself to God as one approved, a workman who does not need to be ashamed and who correctly handles the word of truth"* (2 Timothy 2:15); the responsibility to *"resist the devil, and he will flee from you"* (James 4:7). Then it can be said with Peter, *"For if you do these things, you will never fall"* (2 Peter 1:10).[11]

In Summary (Students)
The statements "a" through "f" relate to doctrine eight.

a. Forgiveness of sins is sometimes called "justification."[1]

b. God forgives differently from man. Man forgives the penalty and forgets the sin or wrongdoing. God paid the penalty on the cross, and therefore can forgive the sin.[2]

c. Forgiveness or remission in the biblical sense includes deliverance or release. So when He forgives our sins, God also delivers us from them.[3]

d. Guilt is taken away by God when He forgives us.[4]

e. Grace is God's love at work to benefit the undeserving sinner. It is by grace that we are forgiven, that we are saved.[5]

f. It is God's plan that we shall know when we are saved. He will tell us so.

The statements "g" through "k" relate to doctrine nine.

g. A person is kept by the same means by which he was saved—by an obedient faith in Christ, continued through his lifetime.[6]

h. God has made reassuring promises to the faithful child of God.[7]

i. God has also given grave warnings to the ones who prove unfaithful.[8,9]

j. Best of all, however, the Bible reminds us that the faithful child of God need never backslide, but can rely on God's promises.[10]

35

k. Of course, as may be expected, we have our own responsibilities—to be obedient and to be faithful.[11]

QUESTIONS TO THINK ABOUT

Questions one through three relate to doctrine eight.

1. God loves all people very much. Then why could He not forgive people their sins without His Son having to die on the cross? Was Christ's death really necessary?

2. How do people try to "bribe" God, or try to earn their way into heaven? What does the Bible have to say to such people?

3. You know that you are an American if you were born in this country. (Were you?) You know that you are alive because it hurts when you are pinched. How do you know that you are a Christian?

Questions four through six relate to doctrine nine.

4. Why do you think it is that God doesn't keep all His children so that they are not *able* to fall away and be lost eternally?

5. We are reminded that victorious living depends on continued faith in Christ. What are some of the things which some saved people—including Salvationists—put their trust in, and fail?

6. Do you know someone who used to be a good Christian, with a victorious life and a warm witness, but who is now away from God—a backslider? Stop right now and pray for that person.

STUDENTS' REVIEW
LESSON 7

From the Scriptures given below, find supporting texts for the following tenets of faith:

We are justified by (His) grace: _____

_____

We are justified by (our) faith: _____

_____

He that believes has the witness in himself: _____

_____

Romans 8:16	Romans 5:1
Acts 13:39	Romans 5:15
Ephesians 2:8	1 John 5:10
Romans 3:24	Galatians 3:24
Titus 2:11	

There is *one word* in the ninth doctrine which is included or implied in each of the following Scriptures. Can you discover it? _____

Joshua 1:8	Acts 5:29
1 Samuel 15:22	2 Thessalonians 1:7,8
Matthew 7:21	2 Corinthians 2:9

LESSON 8

LOOKING TO JESUS

Doubtless everyone of us, young and old alike, has a hero. It may not be a particular person, but we have in our mind images of perhaps an outstanding athlete, a triple-tonguing cornetist, or a great civic or world leader. Perhaps we do not even picture just one person, but hold in our minds the idea of heroic figures: an astronaut as conqueror of space; a strong personality who has friends everywhere; a business tycoon who controls a financial empire—someone against whom we measure our lives.

It is good to have a hero, and it is important that the person we admire is the right kind of hero. Some people make terrible mistakes in life by having the wrong kind; but we, as Christians, should have one hero above all others: Jesus Christ, our Lord. We should long to be like Him. That is the logical result of receiving His forgiveness. And this longing to be Christlike is the call to holiness.

OUR TENTH DOCTRINE

The standard for all Christians is *to be like Christ. And that is holiness.* The Bible tells us that the only way to true Godlikeness, true holiness, is by becoming entirely or wholly sanctified. God has made provision for that as stated in our tenth doctrine:

> *We belive that it is the privilege of all believers to be wholly sanctified, and that their whole spirit and soul and body may be preserved blameless unto the coming of our Lord Jesus Christ.*

"Believers" are those who are saved, who have been born again, whose sins are forgiven, and who are the children of God. We believe that it is *their* privilege to be "wholly sanctified." In order to understand this we must have the answer to two questions: What do we mean by being "wholly sanctified?" Why do Christians need this experience? To be wholly sanctified means to be entirely cleansed and separated from all sin, and to be completely dedicated to God's will and purpose for our lives. We Christians need this experience because, although Christ has forgiven us of our sins, we still possess a *sinful nature* which we inherited from Adam. It is like this: A person can be *forgiven* only for *his own sins,* for which he is responsible. We are not responsible for the sin of Adam. We inherited that, and for that we need, not forgiveness, but deliverance, or cleansing, which the Bible calls being "wholly sanctified."[1]

1. *Inherited inclinations to evil.* After conversion, there remain in the heart of the believer inherited inclinations to evil—a tendency to sin, even though he wants to be good. An Indian said, "There are two dogs inside: a bad one and a good one. They fight. If I say 'sic 'em' to one, he wins. If I say 'sic 'em' to the other, he wins. I want to get rid of bad dog."

In the heart of the sincere believer there often is a struggle, a cruel struggle, against evil. Paul, in Romans 7:19, expressed it like this: *"For what I do is not the good I want to do; no, the evil I do not want to do—this I keep on doing."* Maybe you have had that struggle, too. You find two "dogs" battling within. One is good; the other is bad. Sometimes one wins, sometimes the other. The Bible says that we do not need to continue this struggle between the two "principles." One is the ruling principle of God, which we received when we were saved. The other is the ruling principle of sin, which we inherited from Adam. We can be delivered from this struggle through Jesus Christ. Paul tells us this in Romans: *"It is an agonizing situation, and who on earth can set me free from the clutches of my own sinful nature? I thank God there is a way out through Jesus Christ our Lord"* (Romans 7:24,25, Phillips).

In Romans 8:3, Paul gives testimony to that deliverance through the victory of the ruling principle of the Spirit of God over the ruling principle of sin. Speaking of the ruling principle as a law, Paul says (Romans 8:2): *"Because through Christ Jesus the law* (the ruling principle) *of the Spirit of Life set me free from the law* (the ruling principle) *of sin and death."* There came a time in Paul's life when the controlling principle of the Spirit overwhelmed the principle of sin. And this triumph over evil was due to the overwhelming presence of the Holy Spirit, who is the source of power. This deliverance is termed the experience of *entire sanctification.* Paul implied that it happened to him at a given time, in a given place. And it may be so with us!

A great Christian used to testify: "I can go to the dance anytime I want to. I can take a great foaming stein of beer any time I want to. But the fact is, I don't want to. God has taken the 'want to' away." So it is that the higher law utterly defeats the lower law. Do you remember the tale of the alluring sirens who sang so beautifully on the shore so that sailors would steer the ships in their direction and be shipwrecked? Captains of the vessels tried to turn them from their purpose. One put cotton in the sailors' ears to keep out the sound. Another lashed them to the masts. Some thus struggled past the sirens in an agony of conflict. Others failed, and ships were lost. Ulysses, however, solved the problem by securing the services of Orpheus, who presented better, more alluring music than that of the sirens. The sailors lost their interest in the sirens, who, in despair, casts themselves into the sea and, according to Greek mythology, became rocks.

So it is that the higher law of the Spirit of life in Christ Jesus can become so attractive in our hearts that it will overwhelm and utterly defeat the law of sin and death. In the words of the poet:

> *Though great the world's attraction be*
> *I pass contented by;*
> *Gladly I sacrifice their charms*
> *For those enjoyed on high.*

Sometimes, as here, this experience of entire sanctification is known as *deliverance,* being made free. Sometimes it is spoken of as being *cleansed,* being washed. Sometimes it is simply referred to as *being sanctified.* Paul wrote to the Ephesians, *"Christ also loved the Church* (the believers)*, and gave Himself for it; that He might sanctify and cleanse it"* (Ephesians 5:25,26, *KJV*).

2. *Cleansed and sanctified.* You see, Christ knew that not only do the ungodly need to be forgiven and saved, but the saved need to be cleansed and sanctified. So the atonement, Christ's sacrifice on the cross, was for both purposes.

3. *The positive side of sanctification.* The positive side of sanctification must not be overlooked. When God sanctifies His child, He sends a fullness of the Holy Spirit to fill the heart so that there is no room for the sinful nature from which He has delivered or cleansed him.

4. *The power of the Holy Spirit.* A predominant characteristic of the Holy Spirit is power, the ability to do things now. Read Christ's promise in Acts 1:8 *"But you will receive power when the Holy Spirit comes on you."* When the Christian receives the Holy Spirit in His fullness, he receives the power of His presence. This was fulfilled on the day of Pentecost when *"Suddenly . . . all of them were filled with the Holy Spirit"* (Acts 2:2,4). An examination of the book of Acts will disclose Spirit-filled men, living mighty testimonies for the Lord, winning souls, and building the Kingdom of God. That is still God's plan for His Church. May The Salvation Army be in step with it! May we as Christians be cleansed, be filled, and be mighty for the Lord!

5. *Holiness is also known as perfection.* We need to be aware of the fact that this is not perfection of performance or even of character. But it does mean *perfection of love,* of devotion, of surrender. Jesus was setting the standard when He quoted from the Old Testament what He chose to call the first commandment: *"Love the Lord your God with all your heart* and *with all your soul and with all your mind"* (Matthew 22:37).

Holiness, then is bearing in our character the "image" and "likeness" of Christ. But that is the pattern in which God created man in the first place (Genesis 1:26). So isn't it logical—and wonderful—that God has made provision for us again "to be conformed to the likeness of His Son" (Romans 8:29).[3]

6. *The gift of sanctification is conditional.* The gift of sanctification, as every other gift of God's grace, is *conditional:* It depends on the wholehearted cooperation of the person to be benefited. For the child of God, the necessary *conditions* are fourfold: (1) a *conviction* of the need and the possibility of being sanctified; (2) a *renunciation* of all that is sinful; (3) a *consecration* of everything to the will of God; (4) *faith* that God can—and will—sanctify wholly.[4]

In Summary (Students)

a. Christians often have great inner conflicts between good and evil—the principle of the Spirit versus the principle of sin. However, there is a way of victory over this conflict. This victory is known as *entire sanctification.* The victorious life is known as *holiness.*[2]

b. Christ provided this victorious experience for His people in His atoning sacrifice on Calvary, just as much as he provided salvation for the lost.

c. God not only delivers and cleanses our hearts when He entirely sanctifies us; He also fills our hearts with the Holy Spirit.[2]

d. This possession by God the Holy Spirit gives power which enables us to live victoriously, and to effectively witness for Him.

e. This experience is also known as perfect love.[3]

f. The conditions for entire sanctification are: conviction, renunciation, consecration, and faith.[4]

QUESTIONS TO THINK ABOUT

1. In what way does our being descendants of Adam make it necessary for us not only to be forgiven of our sins, but also to be cleansed from a sinful nature?

2. Who is eligible to seek for holiness of heart?

3. What was the twofold purpose of Christ's atoning sacrifice on the cross?

4. How can sanctification help us not to backslide?

STUDENTS' REVIEW
LESSON 8

Choose from among the Scriptures given those that will support the following statements. (Some of the verses may not apply to either one.)

We believe that God's children can be wholly sanctified. _____

_____

We believe that God's children can be kept blameless. _____

_____

        1 Corinthians 1:8
        Romans 10:9
        1 John 1:9
        Proverbs 3:6
        John 17:17
        1 Thessalonians 5:23,24
        Isaiah 55:10,11
        Philippians 2:15

LESSON 9

GOD'S FUTURE PLANS

If we drive a car, we must carefully scan the road ahead of us. That is a necessary rule of safe driving. As we plan our lives, we should look ahead and plan for the future. That is just good common sense. When we think of eternity, most of us have an insatiable curiosity regarding our future life. That is quite natural. Fortunately, God has given us some—not all—of the answers in His Word. This study will help us to learn and understand something about the future life.

OUR ELEVENTH DOCTRINE

We will look at this doctrine, solidly based on God's Word, to help us in our learning process concerning the future life. Our doctrine states:

> *We believe in the immortality of the soul; in the resurrection of the body; in the general judgment at the end of the world; in the eternal happiness of the righteous; and in the endless punishment of the wicked.*

1. *Last things.* Our study of "last things" really commenced with the tenth doctrine which speaks of "the coming of our Lord Jesus Christ" (1 Thessalonians 5:23). We believe in His coming. We look for the personal return of Jesus Christ, which will be the key event of those last days. His coming will be personal, visible, and glorious.[1] The time of His coming nobody knows: *"No one knows about that day or hour, not even the angels in heaven, nor the Son, but only (God) the Father"* (Mark 13:32). But Jesus will come *"in the same way that you saw Him go to heaven"*—that is, in bodily form, and in the clouds. (See Acts 1:9-11 for the exciting description of Jesus' return to the Father and the promise that He will come back again.) He will come in power and glory, as we read in Mark 8:38: *"When He comes in His Father's glory with the holy angels."*[2]

2. *We believe in the immortality of the soul.* This means that we believe that the soul will never cease to exist. Since man was created in the image and likeness of God (see Genesis 1:26,27; 9:6), he was created for immortality, that is, for an unending existence. Jesus recognized this when He declared, *"Do not be afraid of those who kill the body but cannot kill the soul"* (Matthew 10:28).

From the foregoing it is evident that the soul and body are not identical, and that to kill the body does *not* kill the soul. The death of the body is not in any manner the death of the soul, which continues its unending existence. This argument from the words of our Lord is conclusive. How thrilling, and how sobering, to realize that there is something about us that will continue forever, even after death: namely, our immortal soul. And this is the business that we Salvationists are in—the business of saving souls.[3]

43

3. *We believe in the resurrection of the body.* This will occur in connection with the coming of our Lord Jesus. Resurrection means that a "spiritual body" takes the place of the "natural body" and is united with its spirit. This is a teaching of the Old Testament: *"But your dead will live; their bodies will rise . . . the earth will give birth to her dead"* (Isaiah 26:19). This truth is taught even more clearly in the New Testament. Study carefully Jesus' statement regarding the resurrection of all men: *"Those who have done good will rise to live, and those who have done evil will rise to be condemned"* (John 5:28,29). It is a great mystery, but we know that for the righteous, who will be part of the "resurrection of life," it will be a "spiritual" body. A spiritual body is a body suited to life with God in heaven, even as our present physical body is suited to life here on earth. When likening death to the planting of a seed and resurrection to the springing up of a new plant, Paul declared: *"When buried, it is a physical body; when raised, it will be a spiritual body. There is, of course, a physical body, so there has to be a spiritual body"* (1 Corinthians 15:44, *GNB).*

Through His own resurrection, Jesus gave us a confidence, and a pattern for every believer. If your curiosity is aroused, see 1 Corinthians 15:12-20 for a most interesting commentary by Paul.

4. *We believe in the general judgment at the end of the world.* This solemn event is spoken of throughout the Bible. Read Daniel 7:9,10 or Matthew 25:31-46 or Revelation 20:11-15 for some of the descriptions of that awesome and solemn event. Paul declares: *"He has set a day when He will judge the world with justice"* (Acts 17:31). Again the Apostle tells us: *"We will all stand before God's judgment seat . . . Each of us will give an account of himself to God"* (Romans 14:10,12).

Maybe today people seem to "get away with their sins." They don't seem to get caught. They seem to enjoy themselves. First of all, that's not altogether true. People do suffer for their sins here. They don't always "have a good time." Remember that clearly![5]

5. *We believe in the endless punishment of the wicked.* Hell is the place, or state, of final punishment of the wicked who die in their sins. Even though heaven has been prepared for the righteous dead, hell has been prepared, not for the wicked dead, but for the devil and his angels, and for those who choose to cast their life and their lot with them (see Matthew 25:33,34,41). It isn't a case of an angry God throwing rebels into hell; it is really a case of people going to the eternity they have chosen. It is important to realize this truth.

The Bible clearly declares that the punishment will be endless. Jesus' own words describe it as *"eternal punishment"* (Matthew 25:45), and as *"the fire that never goes out"* (Mark 9:43).[6]

6. *We believe in the eternal happiness of the righteous.* We do believe in heaven. Christ told us about it when He said, *"In My Father's house are many rooms; . . . I am going there to prepare a place for you . . . that you also may be where I am"* (John 14:2,3). There are so many things that we do not know about heaven. Paul says: *"No eye*

44

has seen, no ear has heard, no mind has conceived what God has prepared for those who love Him" (1 Corinthians 2:9).

We do know, however, that God himself *"will be with them"* (Revelation 21:3); that Jesus will be there: *"He who sits on the throne will protect them with His presence"* (Revelation 7:15, *GNB);* and that we shall worship Him forevermore (Revelation 7:15; 22:3-5).[7]

Sin or sinners will not be there. The Bible tells us so!

In Summary (Students)

a. Jesus is coming again in a personal, visible, glorious appearance. No one knows when.[1,2]

b. Each of us has an immortal soul which will never die.[3]

c. There will be a resurrection of our bodies, which will be "heavenly" bodies to suit the eternity we shall be in.[4]

d. The day of judgment, which is already on God's calendar, will disclose the choices people have made. Some will be rewarded; others sent to punishment.

e. For some, it will be an endless life of punishment in hell.[6]

f. For others it will be an eternal life of reward and blessing in heaven.[7]

QUESTIONS TO THINK ABOUT

1. In what ways will Jesus' second coming be different from His first coming to earth?

2. In what ways will the purpose of His second coming be different from that of the first coming?

3. What would you say is the difference between a man's body and his soul?

4. Do sinners have an immortal soul? What is the importance of this truth?

STUDENTS' REVIEW
LESSON 9

There are five truths included in our eleventh doctrine:

We believe:
1. In the immortality of the soul;
2. In the resurrection of the body;
3. In the general judgment at the end of the world;
4. In the eternal happiness of the righteous;
5. In the endless punishment of the wicked.

Considering these by number as (1), (2), (3), (4), and (5), match them with the following verses:

( ) Romans 2:16
( ) Revelation 14:10,11
( ) Luke 12:20
( ) 1 Corinthians 15:35,44
( ) Revelation 7:16,17

THE CHRISTIAN CHURCH

WHEN THE CHURCH BEGAN

When Jesus was on earth, He gathered about Him a group of men who were called His "disciples." They went with Him on His travels; they assisted Him whenever they could; but His main purpose in having them with Him was to train them in the work of His Kingdom. They would be ready, then, to carry on His work after His death, resurrection, and ascension. This was the beginning of Christ's Church.[1]

Historically, the Church started at Pentecost (Acts 1,2) when the disciples in Jerusalem were filled with the Holy Spirit and joyously began to proclaim that Jesus was risen from the dead and that He was Lord and Master. The disciples told their story from house to house, had some meals together in groups, and gladly shared their possessions wherever there was need. The unbelieving Jews began to persecute the followers of Jesus. A particular illustration of such persecution was the stoning of Stephen. The persecution caused a scattering of the Christians and an increase in the number of believers who were won to Christianity in many places.

THE PARENT CHURCH FACES DIFFICULTY

The parent church was at Jerusalem. It was hard for the believers there, with their Jewish background, to understand how others might become Christians without first becoming Jews by accepting the Jewish rituals. A conference was held at Jerusalem (see Acts 15), and the leaders decided that this privilege of joining the Church should be extended to all believers without the necessity of going through Jewish ritual, as long as the newcomers maintained certain ethical standards of pure living and separated themselves from idolatry.[2]

The Jewish Church had been tested by the unbelieving Jews. The entire Church—Gentile and Jewish—was soon to be tested by the persecution of Emperor Nero (64 A.D.) who basely accused the Christians of setting fire to Rome, and then killed many of them. Another emperor prohibited Christianity around 80 A.D., and for more than 200 years persecutions were common and tens of thousands of believers died martyrs' deaths.

A CHRISTIAN EMPEROR

Early in the fourth century (311 A.D.), the Emperor Constantine became a Christian, and the Church was then given relief from periodic persecution. The emperor also proclaimed Christianity to be the official religion of the empire.[3]

POWER OF THE CHURCH

Although starting as a simple Christian brotherhood, the Church took on power, with the leaders assuming that power. The bishop at Rome became the center of the power leaders and became known as the "pope," "papa," "father." This power ultimately spoiled the popes, and all kinds of abuses and superstitions crept into the Church until the leaders of the Roman Church became thoroughly corrupt. Needing money to complete St. Peter's Cathedral at Rome, the agents of the pope sold indulgences (pardons for sins, past and future), giving the people the privilege of sinning.[4,5]

ESTABLISHMENT OF PROTESTANTISM

Martin Luther, a devout and honest German monk, protested against the practice of selling indulgences. He was excommunicated by Rome and put out of the Church. Many people thronged to his side and Protestantism became an established arm of the Church. Zwingli in Switzerland, Calvin in Geneva, John Knox in Scotland were other leaders in the Reformation. The Lutheran Church, the Reformed Church, and the Presbyterian Church grew out of this movement. Since then, of course, there have arisen many other denominations, including, in due time, The Salvation Army.[6,7]

In Summary (Students)

a. While Jesus was on earth, He gathered 12 men as His constant companions and as "trainees" to go among the people to preach.[1]

b. With a number of other believers, these apostles received the gift of the Holy Spirit on the day of Pentecost, and the Church was born.[2]

c. Through the New Testament days and the early centuries following, the Church was established in many cities. When Emperor Constantine the Great, in 311 A.D., became a Christian, he proclaimed Christianity to be the state religion.[3]

d. The Church eventually became corrupt allowing superstition and abuses to become common practices. Then, under Martin Luther, in the 16th century, protest was made against this corruption. This protest developed into the Reformation carried out by that part of the Church known as Protestantism.[4,5]

e. Many other denominations have since sprung up, one of which is The Salvation Army.[6,7,8]

QUESTIONS TO THINK ABOUT

1. Why, do you suppose, are there so many denominations today?

2. Is the cause of Christ advanced or hindered by there being so many denominations? Why?

3. What is meant by the "ecumenical movement?"

4. What are some of the "associations" and "councils" of churches which provide for fellowship and cooperation among various denominations?

STUDENTS' REVIEW
LESSON 10

1. Choose one of these verses for each of the following statements:

Ephesians 5:23   1 Corinthians 12:12,27   Colossians 1:18

a. The Christian Church is likened to a *bride,* of which Christ is the bridegroom, and the head (of the household) _____ _____.

b. The Church is also likened to a *body,* of which Christ is the head _____.

c. The Church is also likened unto *"the body of Christ,"* of which we are "members" or parts_____.

2. Read 1 Corinthians 12:12-27 and list the names of the several parts of the body which Paul says we are as Christians, or as Christian denominations.

LESSON 11
THE SACRAMENTS

A. *THE SIGNIFICANCE OF THE SACRAMENTS*

Salvationists are well aware that most churches observe religious ceremonies called sacraments. The Roman Catholic Church observes seven. Most Protestant churches observe two: *baptism* and the *Lord's Supper.* Some churches add a third: *foot washing.* To most Protestants, a sacrament is either a symbol, a memorial, or a testimony; this means that Protestants feel that the sacraments are desirable and helpful but are not *essential* or necessary to salvation, although they may be required for church membership. The Quakers, however, do not see the necessity of the sacraments and do not observe them.[1]

The Salvation Army in no way criticizes, and certainly does not condemn, any church for its practice. It is, however, *The Salvation Army's firm conviction that the ceremonies commonly known as "the sacraments" are not necessary to salvation or essential to spiritual progress and, therefore, we do not observe them.*

B. *BIBLICAL CEREMONIES AND TYPES*

If it is anything, the religion of Jesus is intended to be a *spiritual* religion. For centuries, under the old covenant, the people of God had used ceremonies and types in their worship. There were the temple sacrifices, fasts and feasts, the rites of circumcision, and baptism for the converts to Judaism. But even long before Jesus came to earth, the prophets, such as David, Jeremiah, and Amos, had to warn God's people that these ceremonies were meaningless, and actually unacceptable to God, if the spirit of the worshiper was not right. The ceremonies and the symbols were getting in the way of true worship and defeating their purpose.

It was with this in mind that Jesus declared plainly at the time of the new covenant: *"Yet a time is coming and has now come when the true worshipers will worship the Father in spirit and truth, for they are the kind of worshipers the Father seeks."* Then Jesus added: *"God is spirit, and His worshipers must worship in spirit and in truth"* (John 4:23,24). This is a profoundly important statement, foreseen by the prophets but made final by Jesus. A new hour, a new day, a new covenant had been made. And those who worship Him in spirit and truth, and not by rote, by ceremony, or by sacrament, are those whom the Father sees as His worshipers.

C. *FULFILLMENT IN JESUS*

Furthermore, as Jesus Himself declared on numerous occasions, the types, the sacrifice, the ceremonies, the symbols, were fulfilled in Him. They need not be repeated or continued. The reason is that God Himself is a *spiritual* being. We Salvationists believe Jesus really meant what He said about fulfillment in Him.[2]

D. BAPTISM

It is true that baptism has become a generally observed sacrament and a condition for church membership. Probably many of your friends in other churches have been baptized; perhaps you have been. To many this ceremony is based on the fact that Jesus Himself was baptized. Therefore, it is said we should "follow our Lord in baptism." An examination of the account, in Matthew 3 will, however, indicate that John the Baptist recognized that his baptism by water was less important than, and was to be replaced by, the baptism of Jesus. His baptism is, of course, with the Holy Spirit, and water baptism is only a symbol. John told Jesus frankly that he needed this new baptism which Jesus only could give.

1. *Jesus reinforced baptism by the Holy Spirit.* Jesus Himself reinforced this fact when He declared, just before His ascension: *"For John baptized with water, but in a few days you will be baptized with the Holy Spirit"* (Acts 1:5). We must remember that Jesus Himself did not baptize with water (John 4:2). Paul did not practice water baptism in his ministry as a rule, saying: *"Christ did not send me to baptize* (with water), *but to preach the gospel"* (1 Corinthians 1:17). We, then, in the Army follow the teaching of John the Baptist, and the teaching and example of our Lord Jesus, and of the great evangelist, Paul.

2. *Baptism is mentioned in the great commission.* It is apparent that Paul recognized the baptism mentioned in the great commission of Matthew 28:19,20 to be baptized with the Holy Spirit, for he explained in Ephesians 4:5 that there is "one Lord, one faith;" there is also "one baptism." He explained that the baptism is the baptism with the Holy Spirit, *"For we were all baptized by one Spirit into one body . . . and we were all given the one Spirit to drink"* (1 Corinthians 12:13). With Paul and Jesus we would stress the only uniquely Christian baptism, which indeed was instituted by Christ: the baptism of the Holy Spirit.[3]

Thus, The Salvation Army declares that the sacrament of water baptism is not necessary to salvation, nor commanded by Jesus.[4]

E. THE LORD'S SUPPER

Some of your friends go to churches where they observe the Lord's Supper. Some of you may have gone to such churches and partaken of communion. It is, however, The Salvation Army's firm conviction that the ceremony known as *the sacrament* of the Lord's Supper is not *essential to spiritual progress.* The Church as a whole, although with many variations in form and meaning, celebrates a communion service which is commonly known as "the Lord's Supper" or "communion" but which others call "the mass." This service consists essentially of the eating of a small piece of bread, or wafer, in remembrance of the body of Christ, "broken for you," and of drinking a small glass of grape juice (sometimes sweet and sometimes fermented) in remembrance of His blood "which is shed for you." The authority to do this is found in the six-word statement by Jesus at the time of the last Passover meal which He celebrated with His disciples, as recorded in Luke 22:19, and referred to in 1 Corinthians 11:24: *"Do this in remembrance of Me."*[5]

It is evident that Jesus did not, in fact, inaugurate here or establish a new sacramental ritual. Read these two verses: Luke 22:19,20. He first declared that the Passover supper, which was of the old covenant, was but a symbol of His own death which would seal the new covenant. In the Passover the Jews served unleavened bread and a cup of wine. So Jesus declared prophetically: *"This* (the bread) *is My body given for you . . . This cup is the new covenant in My blood, which is poured out for you"* (Luke 22:19,20). Paul explained later: *"Christ, our Passover lamb, has been sacrificed"* (1 Corinthians 5:7).

Jesus also gave a directive to remember His death whenever we eat and drink: *"Do this in memory of Me."* The Salvationist does this when he "asks the blessing" before eating. Paul presented the same principle to the Corinthians, of remembering the Saviour's death at their *church meals* (1 Corinthians 11:33), which had come to be called "the Lord's Supper" (v.20). But Church history bears out that not during Bible times of the first century was there developed a "Lord's Supper" in the form of a *sacramental* church observance. Nor is there any evidence that our Lord intended such an observance, nor did the early disciples practice it. This sacramental observance was a later development of the second or third century.[6]

F. *THE SALVATION ARMY'S POSITION*

The Salvation Army takes this position, with the Apostle Paul: *"The Kingdom of God is not a matter of eating and drinking, but of righteousness, peace, and joy in the Holy Spirit"* (Romans 14:17). The Army gives heed to Jesus when He proclaims: *"A time is coming and has now come when the true worshipers will worship the Father in spirit and truth, for they are the kind of worshipers the Father seeks"* (John 4:23).[7]

In Summary (Students)

a. Most churches observe two sacraments: baptism and the Lord's Supper.[1]

b. Jesus, however, emphasized that the new covenant was not to be one of ceremonies, forms, or rituals, but one of a *spiritual* approach to a spiritual God.[2]

c. Jesus repeatedly pointed out that the religious rituals or sacraments of the old covenant were fulfilled in Him of whom they were but a type.

d. The only uniquely Christian baptism is the baptism with the Holy Spirit.[3]

e. We Salvationists follow Paul's example in that we *"are not sent to baptize, but to preach the gospel."*[4]

f. As Salvationists, whenever we eat we should obey our Lord's command to remember Christ's atoning sacrifice on the cross.[5,6]

52

g. It is our firm conviction as Salvationists that the sacraments are not commanded by Jesus, nor are they necessary to salvation, or essential for spiritual progress. Therefore, we do not observe them in the Army.[7]

QUESTIONS TO THINK ABOUT

1. Why do you think that Jesus was so anxious to establish a "spiritual" religion to replace the one of rituals and form?

2. What does the baptism with the Holy Spirit bring to the experience of a Christian? Why is it so important?

3. What are some of the ways a Salvationist may have "communion" with God?

STUDENTS' REVIEW
LESSON 11

1. There are two things necessary to salvation, as declared by Jesus (Mark 1:14,15), and by Paul (Acts 20:20,21): _____ _____.

2. Paul points out to the Ephesians (4:5,6) that there is "_____ *Lord,* _____ *faith,* _____ *baptism, and* _____ *God and Father of all . . ."* And then Paul declared in 1 Corinthians 12:13 that the one Christian baptism is that of the _____.

3. Paul further points out: *"The Kingdom of God is not a matter of eating and drinking* (at the dinner table or at the communion service), *but of righteousness, peace, and* _____ *in the Holy Spirit"* (Romans 14:17).

LESSON 12

THE SALVATION ARMY—
YESTERDAY AND TODAY

As you prepare for senior soldiership, and look forward to your enrollment as a soldier, more and more you will think of The Salvation Army as "my Army"—the "church" through which God has called you to serve Him. You should then want to know the Army's history and structure (its pattern of organization). This lesson has been designed to give you the essentials of Army history and organization. It will be a part of your ongoing commitment to continue to dig deeper into the exciting history, so that you can be a soldier who knows his/her Army and how it functions, and sees it as an important part of the Christian Church.

A. *HISTORY—YESTERDAY*

1. *Beginnings in England:* In 1865, William Booth, who was then a Methodist minister, conducted some meetings in the East End of London. His heart was filled with compassion for the lost and wretched people he saw, and he determined to devote his life to their salvation. At first he wanted to carry on this work under the auspices of his own church, but this was not allowed. After discussing this matter with his wife, Catherine, they decided to venture alone, in faith, on this great undertaking.[1]

Starting with street meetings in front of saloons, they were able to make converts in spite of the attacks, taunts, and gibes flung at them. The converts were trained by William Booth to assist him in his work. An old warehouse was secured for indoor gatherings, which were constantly crowded. For some years the work was carried on under the name of "The Christian Mission," but in 1878, the name was changed to "The Salvation Army."[2]

Because of the military significance of the name, a quasi-military (using military ranks and terminology) form of government was set up, with William Booth as "General," and the adoption of a type of uniform patterned on the British military. At the time of the Founder's death in August 1912, officers and soldiers of the Army were preaching salvation in 34 languages in 58 countries and colonies, and had nearly 16,000 officers and cadets. Today the Army serves around the world.

When William Booth was 15 years of age, he resolved: "God shall have all there is of William Booth." Because of that consecration, The Salvation Army was founded and has become a great international organization. Statistics for 1984 reveal that the Army now serves in 85 countries, and preaches the gospel in 112 languages.

2. *Beginnings in the United States:* By the end of 1878, requests were coming from the United States for officers to carry on Salvation Army work which had been temporarily established by Salvationists who had emigrated to America. George Scott Railton, an ardent

advocate for overseas expansion of the Army, pleaded with General Booth in 1880 to allow him to head the contingent being sent to "open fire" in the States. The Army was thus officially established in 1880 by Railton and with him came seven women officers who became popularly known as the "Seven Hallelujah Lassies."[3]

The Army's 104 years in America can be conveniently divided into three significant periods of development:

— 1880 to 1904: the formative era of struggle, hardship, and rapid growth;

— 1904 to 1934: further expansion and gradual, then mass, acceptance following World War I (these were years of great social change and upheaval in America, encompassing the depression and the development of a whole new attitude by government toward the welfare of its citizens).

— 1934 to the Present: A period of broader interweaving of The Salvation Army with other national policy-making and fund-raising agencies, along with wider acceptance of Army personnel and program in the great family of religious and social-welfare organizations.

As the Army became more firmly established in the United States certain phases of its programs, activities, and relationships developed along the following lines.

— the violence of opposition subsided;

— a period of passive acceptance of the Army led to an indifference toward its work and personnel;

— Army leaders devoted their energies to an internal study of the organization in order to improve personnel and program within the Army;

— a gradual widening of public understanding and approval of the Army principles and practices which led to an overwhelming "shock of recognition" following the devoted services of American Salvationists in World War I;

— following the great war, a grateful nation and its leaders, with open hearts and hands, gave generous support to the Army's work as its officers and soldiers served on all fronts of human need, seeking always, as their first principle, to bring men, women, and children into a right relationship with God;

— the development of a body of supporters who assist the Army through membership in such groups as:
* Salvation Army Advisory Boards
* Service Units
* Associations
* Women's Auxiliaries
* Advisory Councils (to groups such as: Boys' Clubs, Day Care Centers, Girl Guards, summer camps, Adult Rehabilitation Centers, etc.).

56

Through the years, Salvation Army methods have, of necessity, changed, but our motivation has remained the same. All of our work must point toward proclaiming and exemplifying Christ, who said, *"But I, when I am lifted up from the earth, will draw all men to Myself"* (John 12:32).

We have celebrated one century of service in the United States and have moved into our second century of service. Now we will consider our Army today in the second half of this lesson.

B. OUR ARMY—AT WORK TODAY

1. *Our Task:* You will see from your studies of the Army's beginnings that our Movement is not just another church. We are, of course, a part of that great body of Christ known as the Christian Church. We must remember, however, that our corps community centers are not only places of worship and fellowship, but they are headquarters of an Army—The Salvation Army. We have many activities and programs in our corps, but our principal task is to bring people to Christ—to get them saved. We seek to reach the unchurched, wherever they may be. Thus our work is a continual outreach—we cannot function just within our own corps community center buildings, or think of them as only for the use of Salvationists. We must *go out* and *reach* the lost with the gospel of Jesus Christ.

2. *Our Program:* In addition to our meetings for worship and fellowship, the Army reaches out into the community through the following, and other programs and activities:

- *Youth:* Junior Soldiers, Corps Cadets, Sunday school, Girl Guards, Sunbeams, Boy Scouts, Adventure Corps, music and drama groups, summer camps, etc.
- *Adults:* Senior Soldiers, Home League, League of Mercy, Men's Fellowship Clubs, local-officer service, teaching positions in the corps, etc.
- *Homeless Unattached Men and Women:* Adult Rehabilitation Centers, Harbor Light Centers (these centers offer many programs to help restore men and women to society).
- *Women:* Homes for unmarried mothers; residences for young businesswomen, also for older women; emergency lodges for women and children.
- *Senior Citizens:* Residences, drop-in centers, day-care centers, summer camp activities, meal services in the home.
- *Social Services:* These departments provide ongoing services to families, youth, single-parent clients, disoriented men, women, and children; seasonal services at Christmas and Thanksgiving with special feeding programs, food supplies, and gifts.

In certain areas of the country there are specialized types of service provided which may not be listed above. The foregoing should, however, give a quite comprehensive idea of the kinds of programs, activities, and services that the Army today provides.

3. *Our Battlefield—the World:* You may know The Salvation Army only from the viewpoint of your local corps or division, but the Army is a worldwide organization, serving (as of 1984) in 85 countries, and preaching the gospel in 112 languages. As we have studied, the Army was founded by William Booth in 1865, and through the years the following structure (organization) has evolved:

—*International Headquarters, London, England:* The General of The Salvation Army lives in London and serves the worldwide Army through International Headquarters.[3]

—*National Headquarters, Verona, New Jersey:* The national *commander* coordinates the work of The Salvation Army in the United States of America.

—*Territorial Headquarters:* There are four THQs in the United States: located in New York City; Chicago, Illinois; Atlanta, Georgia; and Rancho Palos Verdes, California. A *territorial commander* is in command of the Army work in each territory. A *chief secretary* is second-in-command of the Army work in each territory.

—*Departments of Territorial Headquarters:* The program and activities of the Army come under the supervision and co-ordination of the departments of THQ, and a department head is in charge of each department. In addition to the foregoing, there are three administrative officers—Field Secretary for Personnel; Territorial Secretary for Business Administration; Territorial Secretary for Program—and each department head relates, according to his/her work, to one of these.

—*Divisions:* Each territory is divided geographically (usually by states) into divisions. The divisional commander supervises and guides the work of the Army in his/her division.

—*Corps Community Center:* Each corps is the local "arm" of the Army in hundreds of cities. A corps commanding officer supervises the work in his/her city.[4,5,6]

In addition to the foregoing, the Army has a great overseas (missionary) ministry with dedicated officers and lay people serving in many parts of the world to bring the gospel of Jesus Christ to those who have little or no knowledge of Him. The services provided in these overseas territories are almost unlimited, and magazines *(All the World* and others), films, and newsletters are available from your divisional headquarters to provide further information.

Although the Salvation Army flag, uniform, and certain Army symbols and expressions have been, of necessity adapted or modified, to meet the needs of Salvationists in many countries, it is good to know that they remain essentially the same, and are easily recognized around the world. The rank system of officership and the terminology of soldiership is the same. Above all, the underlying spirit of Salvationism that undergirds all Army work—that of love of God and mankind—is the same around the world. We are one Army!

4.*Our Responsibility Today:* Following your enrollment, as you become more and more involved in the activities and programs of your corps, you will begin to understand that the love of Jesus Christ requires you to make an unreserved commitment to His service. This means that you accept responsibility for making the good news of the gospel known, and for giving service in those positions of local officership which your corps officer may ask you to fill. Because Christ has truly saved you, you will want to, indeed, you must, pray and work earnestly to save others.

For the leadership of your corps, however, there must be trained officers to give full-time service to the salvation war. Salvation Army officers are, therefore, trained and commissioned for service. Individuals respond from the corps to God's call to officership, and when accepted for officership by The Salvation Army, their training as cadets includes:

—Two years of intensive training at one of the four Salvation Army Schools for Officers' Training in the United States.

—A comprehensive curriculum including the study of the Bible, doctrine, Church and Army history, instruction in practical areas of preaching, conducting meetings, the art of soul winning, counseling and, above all, the cultivation of the "Army spirit" of love for God and mankind and the self-sacrificial dedication to seeking the lost and building the Kingdom of God on earth. Practical training in community relations, social services and business administration is also a part of the curriculum.

—Field training (practical corps experience) in the corps and community setting, under the supervision of experienced corps officers; and various visitation experiences in homes and institutions.

At the conclusion of their two-year training period, the cadets are commissioned as Salvation Army officers, ordained as ministers, and sent to their first appointments. From that point, they carry all the rights and privileges of ministers, such as performing wedding ceremonies, conducting funerals, representing The Salvation Army as a particular branch of the Christian Church, serving in the chaplaincy, and other duties which they may be expected to fulfill. The Salvation Army is a recognized denomination, and for the purpose of holding property and estates it is incorporated in the United States of America.[8]

5. *Ceremonies and Terminology:* The Salvation Army has its own distinctive ceremonies and terminology for suitable, special occasions. Following are descriptions of these:

Ceremonies

Dedication Service: During the dedication of a child, water is not used, but the child is presented to the Lord with a strict charge to the parents to rear him/her in the way of the Lord.

Enrollment of Soldiers: At the time of enrollment (also referred to as "swearing in" of soldiers), the recruit becomes a full member of The Salvation Army, pledging to be faithful to the *Articles of War* which he/she has signed.

Weddings: The Army has well-arranged *Articles of Marriage* which help those entering into marriage to fulfill the purpose of the wedding. Salvationists who are married in uniform, standing beneath the flags, fulfill the Salvation Army practice of simplicity and witness. Salvationists recognize a wedding as a sacred event, and thus secular songs and frivolous customs should be avoided.

Funerals: Death for a Salvationist is referred to as "promotion to Glory." The funeral arrangements do not, through any detail, express the hopelessness of those who do not know the risen Christ. Instead of black, the Army's funeral color is white, and the flags are draped with white ribbons. Soldiers are expected to attend the funeral in uniform and may, if they wish, wear a white ribbon band around the sleeves of their tunics. A memorial service for the promoted comrade may be held later, during a Sunday service, and the theme should be thankfulness for the life of the comrade and praise for God's grace in Christ.

Terminology

Soldier: An individual who has been soundly converted, has fulfilled the requirements of soldiership preparation, has signed the *Articles of War,* and has been enrolled under the flags.

Penitent-form: This form (structure, or bench) at the front of the platform is also known as the altar. It provides a place for the penitent sinner, and the Christian, to kneel and seek through prayer the fulfillment of his/her needs. The penitent-form is not the only place to meet God, but it gives the seeker opportunity to make a public confession, and to receive wise counseling.

Holiness Table or Altar: Usually this is a table with a special cloth covering, placed at the center of the front of the Army hall, in front of the penitent-form. It is provided as a place of prayer for those seeking the blessing of holiness (sanctification), which we have previously considered. This also is not the only place where holiness can be received, but it serves the purpose as a place of public confession and counseling.

Uniform: An official Salvation Army uniform for both soldiers and officers may be secured from the Supplies and Purchasing Department in your territory. Wearing a uniform identifies you as a Salvationist and gives opportunity for special, public witness for God. It is a distinct honor to be allowed to wear Army uniform, and it must never be worn unworthily.

World Services (Self Denial): Emerging from the early days of the

Army, this term is the designated name of the Army's overseas (missionary) financial effort. All soldiers are encouraged to contribute a set amount each week (in your cartridge envelope) specifically for Self-Denial giving, so that a final ingathering of funds at Easter may be celebrated.

Harvest Festival: A financial effort launched each autumn through the corps to assist in the training of Salvation Army officers. All money secured through this effort is channeled into the budget of the School for Officers' Training in your territory.

Knee Drill: A special prayer meeting.

Fishing: Moving among the congregation and speaking to the people about coming to the penitent-form.

Testimony: A brief, personal witness, either in or out of meetings, as to what God has done for the saved person.

Firing a Cartridge: Giving a weekly tithe for the support of God's work through the corps. This should be placed in the offering each Sunday in an appropriate envelope known as a "cartridge."

Meetings: The Army's "services" held especially for worship and Christian fellowship.

Open-air Meeting: Street meeting held to preach the gospel to those who may not otherwise be reached for Christ.

Army Symbols

Flag: The Salvation Army *flag* (yellow, red and blue), is the same in every country where the Army serves. The *red* background represents the blood of Jesus Christ: *yellow* symbolizes the fire of the Holy Spirit; *blue* border stands for purity of life and spirit. The flag is displayed in every Army building and is carried at the head of the march in every country where the Army serves.

Crest: The Army crest is worn by men and boys on their Army caps, and is part of the insignia worn on the uniforms of officers of certain ranks. It appears on or in all Salvation Army publications, including the front of our *Song Book.* The *sun* on the crest represents the light and fire of the Holy Spirit; the *cross* is the symbol of the cross of Christ; the *"S"* stands for salvation; the *swords* are symbols of the sword of the Spirit; the *shots* remind Salvationists of the truths of the gospel. The crest is an international symbol and is capped with a crown, representing the "crown of life."[9]

In Summary (Students)

a. Under the leadership of William Booth the Army started as a street mission in East London in 1865.[1]

b. This movement, gaining momentum during the intervening years, became known in 1878 as The Salvation Army, and is now in operation around the world.[2]

c. Opening fire in the United States in 1880, The Salvation Army is now administered in four territories and numerous divisions, all under the supervision of the International Headquarters in London, England.[3]

d. Each territory also has numerous departments for specialized administration.[4,5]

e. Every corps is comprised of several departments and its program is carried out by various local officers with the general leadership of the corps officer.[6]

f. The Salvation Army is international in its services, under many national flags, in many languages, and is at work in many overseas countries. But it is all one Army.[7]

g. Salvation Army officers are trained in a two-year program geared to preparing them for carrying on the Army's work.[8]

h. The Salvation Army has numerous distinctive ceremonies and terms which are best suited to its unique place in the community of Christian organizations.[9]

i. The Salvationist is committed, with the Army, to proclaim salvation from sin to every sinning soul, and also to make others happier and better through his/her Christian service.

j. The spirit of Salvationism leads the Salvationist into the pulpit and out onto the street corner to proclaim Christ to all who come under his/her ministry.[10]

QUESTIONS FOR DISCUSSION

1. It has been said that The Salvation Army is "a long shadow of William Booth." Do you agree or disagree with this statement? Why?
2. In view of your studies of Salvation Army history and doctrine, tell whether or not you think "The Salvation Army" is a good name for our Movement.
3. How does uniform wearing help a Salvationist?
4. In what ways is the Army different from most churches?
5. You are soon to be enrolled as a soldier: in what ways will the Army be your church?
6. Do you believe that your corps is fulfilling the purposes of The Salvation Army as it serves the people of your community? Give reasons for your answer.
7. List some reasons for the Army's overseas (missionary) work, and tell what your corps is doing to help the Army's worldwide ministry.
8. How is a Salvation Army officer similar to and different from a minister of a church?

STUDENTS' REVIEW
LESSON 12

Draw and complete a diagram of one of the following:

—The chain of command from the General to the soldier.

—The territorial organization of your territory including the offices of the territorial commander, chief secretary, three cabinet members, departments, divisions, and corps. Insert the names of all persons involved in leadership in these positions and offices.

—The organization of your corps showing the programs and activities and the relationship of the local officers to the corps departments. List the names and positions of the local officers in your corps.

No diagrams are required for the following, but you are to select one of the suggestions, complete it and hand it to your corps officer, or other person who may instruct your class:

—Present some divisional, territorial, and national facts regarding The Salvation Army as listed in the *Disposition of Forces,* or other sources.

—Report on a certain aspect or department of The Salvation Army as related to some special service or purpose (e.g., tell about the work of the Men's Social Service Department; the Youth Department, etc.).

—Learn about and report on the training of Salvation Army officers in your territory. (If possible, secure from Supplies & Purchasing Department a copy of *A Modern Pilgrim's Progress*—the story of Salvation Army officership).

LESSON 13

SALVATIONISM
The Articles of War

In addition to our statement of faith in the cardinal doctrines, The Salvation Army has a document, known as the *Articles of War,* which must be subscribed to and signed by every recruit before being enrolled as a senior soldier. The following is a summary of what the articles provide:

a. They give personal witness to salvation and a pledge to lifelong faithfulness to God.

b. They express confidence in and a pledge to The Salvation Army as being God's Army.

c. They include a brief summary of Salvation Army doctrine.

The articles can easily be divided into two sections. Section One covers the above summary. Section Two contains eight paragraphs: the first five speak of the Salvationist's commitment to God; the last three declare his/her commitment to The Salvation Army. We will study the second section under those two divisions.[1]

A. *THE SALVATIONIST'S COMMITMENT TO GOD*

1. "Therefore, I do here and now, and forever, renounce the world with all its sinful pleasures, companionships, treasures, and objects, and declare my full determination boldly to show myself a soldier of Jesus Christ in all places and companies no matter what I may have to suffer, or lose, by so doing."

The salvation soldier should abstain from all worldliness. Jesus warned against this when He said: *"What good will it be for a man if he gains the whole world, yet forfeits his soul?"* (Matthew 16:26); and again: *"The seed that fell among thorns stands for those who hear, but as they go on their way they are choked by life's worries, riches and pleasures, and they do not mature"* (Luke 8:14). See also: Paul (Colossians 3:2); and John (1 John 2:15), for these also add their warnings.[2]

2. "I do here and now declare that I will abstain from the use of all intoxicating liquor, from the use of tobacco in any form, and from the nonmedical use of all addictive drugs."

Because of the terrible toll on health and usefulness, and of life itself, the Salvationist will continue to take this tremendously important stand against intoxicating liquors and destructive drugs. Since the effects of alcoholic beverages come by willful indulgence, and need the grace of God for full deliverance, The Salvation Army sees alcoholism as *both* a disease and a sin. We take our stand as possibly the largest international movement against even social drinking. In like fashion, the Army wages a continual war against the mounting scourge of addictive and destructive drugs which are engulfing society. We take a militant stand against the use of tobacco. Recent scientific conclusions support the Army's consistent contention through the years regarding the destructive effect of tobacco in its various forms. We remember that our *"bodies are members of Christ Himself"* (1 Corinthians 6:15); *"a temple of the Holy Spirit, who is in you"* (v.19). We remember that we are bought with a price, so we must use our bodies for God's glory (vv.19,20). We should, therefore, as Paul says, *"offer your bodies as living sacrifices, holy and pleasing to God"* (Romans 12:1).[3]

3. "I do here and now declare that I will abstain from the use of all low or profane language; from the taking of the name of God in vain; and from all impurity; or from taking part in any unclean conversation, or the reading of any obscene book or paper at anytime, in any company, or in any place."

The Salvationist should shun swearing or profanity of every kind. The Bible says: *"You shall not misuse the name of the Lord your God, for the Lord will not hold anyone guiltless who misuses His name"* (Exodus 20:7). This includes slang, much of which is merely a cover for swearing.[4] In a day of loose morals and obscene literature, the Salvationist should always be on guard against being a party to this kind of thing. And, of course, to "misuse the name of the Lord your God" also refers to hypocritical profession and insincere prayer. God's name *is* holy. It must not be used by Salvationists lightly or in any unworthy fashion.[5]

4. "I do here declare that I will not allow myself in any falsehood, deceit, misrepresentation, or dishonesty; neither will I practice any fraudulent conduct in my business, my home, nor in any other relationship in which I may stand to my fellowmen, but I will deal truthfully, fairly, honorably, and kindly with all those who may employ me, or whom I may myself employ."

Honesty is not only the best policy, it is God's unaltered standard. Read the above statement again, and add "in my school," "in my play," "in my work." Paul prayed for his people: *"Now we pray to God that you will not do anything wrong"* (2 Corinthians 13:7).[6]

5. "I do here declare that I will never treat any woman, child, or other person, whose life, comfort, or happiness may be placed within my power, in an oppressive, cruel or cowardly manner, but that I will protect such from evil and danger, so far as I can, and promote to the utmost of my ability, their present welfare and eternal salvation."

A Salvationist's attitude toward others is evidence of his religious experience. It is through us that others see God.[7] In addition to this, as Salvationists we will realize that our commitment to God must also be made in other areas. Bible reading, for example, is of prime importance. Jesus said: *"You diligently study the Scriptures . . . These are the Scriptures that testify about Me"* (John 5:39).[8]

The study of God's Word is of tremendous importance to the Salvationist's devotional life. We must learn to blend our spirits with God's Spirit in the close communion which comes from daily periods set aside for meditation and prayer. Nothing must be allowed to get in the way of our communion with God. We live or die as Christians by our faithfulness to this practice. The Word says: *"Look to the Lord and His strength; seek His face always"* (1 Chronicles 16:11).

The Salvationist also will *"grow in the grace and knowledge of our Lord and Saviour Jesus Christ"* (2 Peter 3:18).[9]

It is wonderful to be a babe in Christ—a new Christian. But you would not want to be a baby throughout all of your life. The spiritual food you will get from your Bible reading and devotions will provide your vitality, and being active for God will provide the exercise.

B. *THE SALVATIONIST'S COMMITMENT TO THE ARMY*

6. "I do here declare that I will spend all the time, strength, money, and influence I can in supporting and carrying on this war, and that I will endeavor to lead my family, friends, neighbors, and all others whom I can influence, to do the same, believing that the sure and only way to remedy all the evils in the world is by bringing men and women to submit themselves to the government of the Lord Jesus Christ."

Wholehearted Salvationists are needed! In this war there can be no compromise, no halfhearted measures. Good Salvationists will be dependable in their attendance at meetings, and they will not confine their attendance to just one meeting a week. They will not attend merely to worship, but will endeavor, through their faith and efforts, to bless others and to win souls. As Paul wrote: *"Let us consider how we may spur one another on toward love and good deeds. Let us not give up meeting together, as some are in the habit of doing, but let us encourage one another—and all the more as you see the day* (of judgment) *approaching"* (Hebrews 10:24,25).[11]

Then there is the matter of giving. All Salvationists should support their corps. While a tithe may not be binding, it is a good measure which many follow. This means that for every ten dollars you earn, or receive, one dollar should be set aside for the Lord. God's Word says: *"Bring the whole tithe into the storehouse, that there may be food in My house. 'Test Me in this,' says the Lord Almighty, 'and see if I will not throw open the floodgates of heaven and pour out so much blessing that you will not have room enough for it'"* (Malachi 3:10).[12]

7. "I do declare that I will always obey the lawful orders of my officers, and that I will carry out to the utmost of my power all the orders and regulations of the Army; and further that I will be an example of faithfulness to its principles, advance to the utmost of my ability its operations, and never allow, where I can prevent it, any injury to its interest, or hindrance to its successes."

Loyalty is one of the most urgent demands made upon a Salvationist. There will be those who criticize the Army, its leaders, and its program, but there will always be areas in which the Army should improve. Every soldier, however, owes loyalty to his/her leaders, to the corps, and to fellow Salvationists. Paul gave good advice when he said: *"Now we ask you, brothers, to respect those who work hard among you, who are over you in the Lord and who admonish you. Hold them in the highest regard in love because of their work. Live in peace with each other"* (1 Thessalonians 5:12,13).[13]

8. "And I do here and now call upon all present to witness that I enter into this understanding, and sign these *Articles of War* of my own free will, feeling that the love of Christ who died to save me requires from me this devotion of my life to His service for the salvation of the whole world, and therefore I wish now to be enrolled as a soldier of The Salvation Army."[14]

STUDENTS' REVIEW
LESSON 13

Study carefully, and pray about your *Articles of War* which have been presented to you.

Be sure that you understand each part and, in the will of God, be prepared to sign your copy of the *Articles of War* at the consecration service which will be held at the completion of this course.

Also read carefully and prayerfully *Chosen To Be a Soldier,* orders and regulations for soldiers of The Salvation Army.

READING AND REFERENCE LIST

Agnew, Milton S. *More Than Conquerors* (holiness of heart and life as presented in the book of Romans). Kansas City, Missouri: Beacon Hill Press, 1977.

Agnew, Milton S. *The Holy Spirit: Friend and Counselor.* Kansas City, Missouri: Beacon Hill Press, 1980.

Agnew, Milton S. *Transformed Christians.* Kansas City, Missouri. Beacon Hill Press, 1974.

Agnew, Milton S. *The Security of the Believer* (booklet). Self published, 1974.

Booth, William. *Purity of Heart* (reprint). Oakville, Ontario, Canada: Triumph Press, 1982.

Brengle, Samuel Logan. *Heart Talks on Holiness; Helps to Holiness; Love Slaves; Resurrection Life and Power; The Guest of the Soul; The Soul-Winner's Secret; The Way of Holiness; Wait on the Lord; When the Holy Ghost Is Come.* The Salvation Army, various dates.

Bramwell-Booth, Catherine. *Catherine Booth.* London: Hodder and Stoughton, 1970.

Brown, Colin, ed. *Dictionary of New Testament Theology.* (3 Volumes, excellent reference work; thoroughly evangelical). Grand Rapids: Zondervan.

Burrows, William. *All Things New* (reprint). New York: The Salvation Army, 1977.

Burrows, William. *The Mercy Seat* (reprint). New York: The Salvation Army, 1977.

Collier, Richard. *The General Next to God.* London: Fontana/Collins, 1968.

Coutts, Frederick. *No Discharge in This War* (a one-volume history of The Salvation Army). New York: The Salvation Army (by special permission of Hodder and Stoughton, Ltd.), 1975. Originally published in London in 1965.

Coutts, Frederick. *Siempre En Pie De Guerra* (Spanish edition of *No Discharge in This War).* London: The Salvation Army, 1975. Printed in Spain.

Coutts, Frederick. *T he Call to Holiness* (reprint). London: The Salvation Army, 1977.

Coutts, Frederick. *The Splendour of Holiness.* London: The Salvation Army, 1983.

Coutts, John. *This We Believe.* London. The Salvation Army, 1976.

Chesham, Sallie. *Peace Like a River* (the life of Commissioner Samuel Logan Brengle). Atlanta, Georgia: The Salvation Army, 1981.

Chesham, Sallie. *Preaching Ladies* (the story of Eliza Shirley, her family, and "preaching ladies" in Great Britain and the United States). New York: The Salvation Army, 1983.

Field, Benjamin. *Handbook of Theology.* Freeport, Pa.: The Fountain Press, 1949.

Henry, Carl F. H. *Basic Christian Doctrines.* New York: Holt, Rinehart, and Winston, 1962.

McKinley, Edward H. *Marching to Glory* (the history of The Salvation Army in the United States). San Francisco: Harper & Row, 1980.

Metcalf, William. *Another Pentecost?* London: The Salvation Army, 1973.

Metcalf, William. *The Salvationist and the Sacraments.* London: The Salvation Army, 1965.

Morris, Henry M. *The Genesis Record.* Grand Rapids, Michigan: Baker Book House, 1976.

Payne, J. Barton. *The Theology of the Old Testament:* Grand Rapids, Michigan: Zondervan, 1962.

Read, Edward. *Studies in Sanctification.* Toronto, Canada: The Salvation Army, 1975.

The Salvation Army. *Chosen To Be a Soldier* (Orders and Regulations for soldiers of The Salvation Army). London: The Salvation Army, 1977.

The Salvation Army. *Handbook of Doctrine.* London: The Salvation Army, 1969.

The Salvation Army. *Heritage of Holiness* (a compilation of papers on the historical background of holiness teaching). New York: The Salvation Army, 1977.

The Salvation Army. *The Doctrine We Adorn* (an abridged study of Salvation Army doctrines). London: The Salvation Army, 1969.

The Salvation Army. *The Sacraments—the Salvationist's Viewpoint.* London: The Salvation Army, 1965.

The Salvation Army. *Year Book.* Published once a year in London.

Sandall, Robert. *The History of the Salvation Army.* London: Thomas Nelson and Sons, Ltd., 1947.

Troutt, Margaret. *The General Was a Lady.* Nashville: A.J. Holman Company, 1980.

Waldron, John D. *G.S.R.* (a view of Commissioner George Scott Railton). Oakville, Ontario, Canada: The Salvation Army, Triumph Press, 1981.

Waldron, John D. *The Privilege of All Believers* (an anthology on the doctrine of holiness). Oakville, Ontario, Canada: The Salvation Army, 1982.

Waldron, John D. *The Salvationist and the Atonement* (an anthology). Oakville, Ontario, Canada: The Salvation Army, Triumph Press, 1983.

Waldron John D. *Women in The Salvation Army* (an anthology). Oakville, Ontario, Canada: The Salvation Army, Triumph Press, 1983.

Watson, Bernard. *Soldier Saint* (George Scott Railton). Reprint in paperback: New York: The Salvation Army, 1977.

Wiley, H. Orton. *Christian Theology* (3 Volumes). Kansas City: Beacon Hill Press, 1967.

While women weep, as they do now,
    I'll fight;
While little children go hungry, as they do now,
    I'll fight;
While men go to prison, in and out, as they do now,
    I'll fight;
While there is a poor lost girl upon the streets,
While there remains one dark soul without the light of God,
    I'll fight—I'll fight to the very end!

—William Booth